Egyptian
Myths

To my mother and father

THE · LEGENDARY · PAST

Egyptian
Myths

GEORGE HART

Published for The Trustees of

The British Museum by

BRITISH MUSEUM 𝕀𝕀𝕀𝕀𝕀𝕀 PRESS

© 1990 The Trustees of the British Museum
Seventh impression 1999
Published by British Museum Press
a division of The British Museum Company Ltd.
46 Bloomsbury Street, London WC1B 3QQ

British Library Cataloguing in Publication Data
Hart, George, 1945–
    Egyptian myths. – (The legendary past.)
    1. Egyptian myths & legends, ancient periods
    I. Title
    398.20932
    ISBN 0-7141-2064-2

Designed by Gill Mouqué
Cover design by Slatter-Anderson

Set in 10½ pt Sabon and printed in Great Britain
by The Bath Press, Bath

*FRONT COVER The god Horus
with the ring of eternity
in its claws.*

Mountains near the turquoise-mines of Maghara in the Sinai peninsula. The turquoise mined here decorated hair pendants of the sort lost by one of the harem-rowers in Tales of Fantasy.

Contents

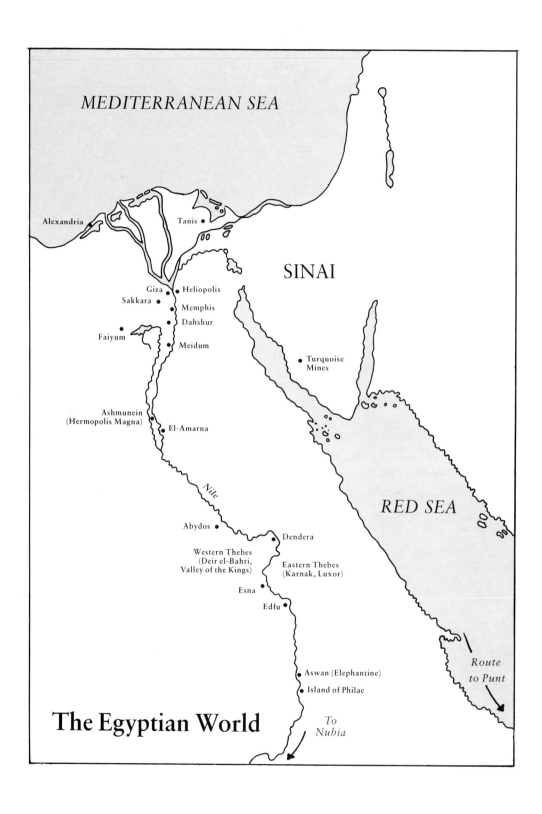

MEDITERRANEAN SEA

Alexandria •

Tanis •

SINAI

Giza • • Heliopolis
Sakkara •
Memphis
Dahshur
Faiyum •
• Meidum

• Turquoise
Mines

Ashmunein
(Hermopolis Magna) •
• El-Amarna

Nile

RED SEA

Abydos •
• Dendera

Western Thebes
(Deir el-Bahri,
Valley of the Kings)

Eastern Thebes
(Karnak, Luxor)

Esna •
Edfu •

• Aswan (Elephantine)
• Island of Philae

*Route
to Punt*

The Egyptian World

*To
Nubia*

Introduction

Egyptian mythology is a rich and perplexing panorama of visual and written images. In an attempt to clarify some aspects, I have divided the subject into two broad categories. The most manageable material is quite straightforward and includes the tales and legends involving escapism to exotic lands, amusement at the exploits of magicians and the apotheosis of historical heroes.

The other category is what I venture to call 'myths of the higher consciousness'. My personal view is that these formed an active, integral element in ancient Egyptian government and society; they are far from being a series of fossilised *mémoires* on gods and goddesses. Those concerning the origins of the cosmos, the concept of lawful succession to the throne and the vision of a regenerative journey made by the sun at night, stand out as the projections of the ancient Egyptians' thoughts, hopes and fears about the human condition and the troubles experienced in the course of one lifetime.

Investigation of natural phenomena and confrontation with the 'mysterious' mattered deeply to the ancient Egyptians, even if there was not always an explanation and if the result was occasionally incomprehensible and contradictory. Consequently, metaphysical myths of creation and magical formulae directed against the forces of chaos – manifest in the threat of the underworld snake Apophis – signify the ancient Egyptian quest for ultimate knowledge. This is echoed in what has been called the modern dilemma:

'We shall not cease from exploration
And the end of all our exploring
Will be to arrive where we started
And know the place for the first time . . . '
(from T. S. Eliot, *Little Gidding*)

But it is not only on modern times that Egyptian myths have left their mark. Throughout the last two and a half thousand years, foreign visitors to the Nile Valley have recorded their reactions to the vast pantheon of deities inscribed on tombs, temples and papyri. Herodotus, the fifth-century Greek historian and ethnographer, gives some accounts of Egyptian religion but is respectfully reticent about divulging sacred rites:

I have held converse with the priests of Hephaistos [Ptah] at Memphis. I went to Thebes and to Heliopolis intent on discovering if the information I gathered in Memphis would be verified, since the Heliopolitans are regarded as the wisest of Egyptians. As to their explanations of the 'sacred', I am not keen on fully disclosing that knowledge except perhaps in giving the names of certain rituals which I consider to be already 'common currency' among men.
(*Histories* II, chapter 3)

In a similar vein are the comments by the entertaining novelist Apuleius, who has his hero Lucius undergo degrading adventures while in the form of an ass, and who Isis transforms as an initiate into her mysteries. In contrast, however, the xenophobic Roman satirist Juvenal openly mocks Egyptian beliefs and scorns the cult of Isis. Even ordinary tourists in late antiquity have left their impressions (unforgivably as graffiti) about Egypt's complex mythology: 'I, Dioskorammon, looked upon this nonsense and found it bewildering!' (scratched on the wall of the tomb of Ramesses VI in the Valley of the Kings).

But Egyptian myths, though seemingly outlandish to some, have survived because the society out of which they originated considered them crucial to the creation of a view of the world. Scribes, priests and story-tellers transmitted myths to explain aetiological phenomena, to provide data for the continuity of existence in the afterlife and to exhibit the versatility of their imaginations. So whether as part of a religious quest or anthropological investigation or whether for an adventure into the surreal, the myths and legends of ancient Egypt leave us richer for their speculation and imagery.

Pectoral of princess Sit-Hathor-Yunet depicting in gold and semi-precious stones two falcons flanking the cartouche of Senwosret II (1897–1878 BC). The princess' royal name, Kha-Kheperre, involves the image of the scarab beetle and the sun's rays breaking out on the eastern horizon at dawn.

Creation legends

The creation of the world, by whom and how, were subjects of constant interest to the Egyptians. Three cosmogonies were formulated based upon the traditions of three ancient cities – Heliopolis, Hermopolis and Memphis.

Major sources

At the outset of this book we must plunge deep into documents crucial to our understanding of the ancient Egyptian view of the cosmos. Columns of hieroglyphs were carved 4,300 years ago in the vestibule and sarcophagus hall of the pyramid of King Wenis (*c.* 2350 BC) at Sakkara, necropolis of the royal capital of Memphis, with the intention of securing a hereafter for the monarch in the vicinity of the sun god. Subsequent rulers of the Old Kingdom (*c.* 2649–2152 BC) continued this tradition. Known as *Pyramid Texts*, this corpus of spells and speculations gives us the opportunity to evaluate the complex imagery centred upon the Egyptian pantheon. It also forms the earliest religious compilation in the world.

In the next major era of Egyptian civilisation, called the Middle Kingdom (2040–1783 BC), we find that the prerogatives of royalty in defining status in the afterlife through magical inscriptions were usurped by provincial governors and court dignitaries. Their coffins became supernatural caskets painted with funerary formulae addressed to Anubis and Osiris, amuletic 'Eyes of Horus', luxury goods, basic rations, hundreds of tightly written spells (published by Egyptologists under the title *Coffin Texts*) and maps of the netherworld – all designed to neutralise the forces of chaos and to fortify the owner's spirit with hopes of joining the sun god's entourage. Scattered throughout these *Pyramid* and *Coffin Texts* can be found vital comments about the myth of the creator god of Heliopolis, provided of course you control your frustration at the ancient Egyptian editor's scorn for sustained logical analysis. Much later in date, at the beginning of the third century BC, a British Museum papyrus (also known as Papyrus Bremner-Rhind), traces by means of graphic phraseology the development of life from the creator god. (Although Ptolemaic in date this papyrus is likely to have evolved from an original written down at least a thousand years earlier.)

For the survival of the metaphysical account of creation by Ptah, god of Memphis, we are indebted to King Shabaka (712–698 BC), who belonged

The Shabaka stone bearing an inscription carved around 700 BC which is our main source for the metaphysical creation myth devised by the priests of Ptah at Memphis. It was supposedly saved by order of King Shabaka but subsequently used as a mill-stone.

to the expansionist Nubian dynasty whose capital was near Gebel Barkal in the Sudan. He followed up the invasion of Memphis of his predecessor Piye (formerly read Piankhi) with a more permanent occupying force. On a tour of inspection of the Temple of Ptah, Shabaka was horrified to discover that its most sacred papyrus scroll, containing a drama version of the accession of the god Horus to the throne of Egypt and the Memphite myth of the creator god, was being devoured by worms. He immediately ordered that the remaining undamaged text of the scroll be incised on a slab of black granite. His pious intentions, however, were partially thwarted: prior to its acquisition by the British Museum, the 'Shabaka Stone' was used as a mill-stone, as the deep gouge in its centre and the radials emanating from it testify.

Early scholars studying the original date of the 'Memphite theology' copied onto the stone believed that the language of the text pointed towards an Old Kingdom prototype. More careful scrutiny of the epithets of Ptah and the thought structure has led to the rejection of a date in the third millennium BC in favour of a Ramesside (c. 13th century BC) or later origin of this remarkable myth.

Our evidence for Amun as the creator god of Hermopolis rests primarily on Papyrus Leiden I 350, a vast encomium of the god emphasising his exclusive, procreative role. In addition, the New Kingdom temples of Deir el-Bahri and Luxor reveal Amun deserting his mysterious confines in the sky for sexual union with the reigning queen of Egypt, thereby fathering the future monarch. Finally, in the Graeco-Roman era, the last centuries of temple decoration in Egypt, such as at Esna and Edfu, when priestly scribes often gave obscure and enigmatic theological compositions to the sculptors to carve, the hiero-glyphs preserve accounts of creation which are imaginative and rich in subtle allusions but seem to have lost direction in terms of cosmic revelation.

The sun god of Heliopolis

Under the suburbs of north-east Cairo lie the ruins of Yunu, once counted among the foremost and most ancient sanctuaries in Egypt. It was known as Heliopolis, or City of the Sun, to Herodotus, the Greek historian who visited the region in the fifth century BC, well over two thousand years after the first dedications had been made at its shrines. Here the intellectuals at the time of the unification of Upper and Lower Egypt (*c.* 3000 BC) began to formulate a cosmogony to explain the vital elements of their universe, culminating in their significant input into the *Pyramid Texts* of Dynasties V and VI.

Before the development of a structured cosmos there existed in darkness a limitless ocean of inert water. It was envisaged as the primeval being called Nu or Nun. No temples were ever built to honour it, but the nature of Nu is present in many cult sanctuaries in the form of the sacred lake which symbol-ises the 'non-existence' before creation. In fact, this vast expanse of lifeless water never ceased to be and after creation was imagined to surround the celestial firmament guarding the sun, moon, stars and earth as well as the boundaries of the underworld. There was always a fear in the Egyptian mind that Nu would crash through the sky and drown the earth. Such a destruction is hinted at in Spell 1130 of the *Coffin Texts* in Faulkner's 1973 edition where we read: 'mounds will be cities and cities become mounds and mansion will destroy mansion'. When this *Götterdämmerung* ('twilight of the gods') occurs the only survivors will be the gods Atum and Osiris in the form of snakes, 'unknown to mankind and unseen by other gods'.

Atum, 'lord of Heliopolis' and 'lord to the limits of the sky', constitutes the demiurge, the creator of the world, who rose out of Nu at the beginning of time to create the elements of the universe. As the sun god, he self-developed into a being and stood on a raised mound, an image suggestive of the banks and islands that re-emerge after the season of the Nile inundation. (It was natural that the régime of the River, source of Egypt's life and prosperity, should influence the concepts of creation just as the early scribes' environment dictated the signs of the hieroglyphic script.) This primeval mound became formalised as the *Benben*, a firm pyramidal elevation to support the sun god; the actual stone relic, perhaps regarded as the petrified semen of Atum, was alleged to survive in the *Hewet-Benben* (Mansion of the Benben) in Heliopolis.

The underlying notion of the name Atum is one of totality, thus as the sun god he is the *Monad*, the supreme being and quintessence of all the

The sun god Re-Horakhti before the Benben (primeval mound) of Heliopolis. Pyramidion of Ramose from Deir el-Medina, c. 1300 BC.

forces and elements of nature. Therefore, he contains within himself the life-force of every other deity yet to come into being. In Egyptian thought totality had a positive power, as in the idea of completing an eternity of existence, and a destructive aspect, as in consigning an enemy to the flames. This dualism inherent in the Monad allows for the future birth of a constructive goddess such as Isis as well as a god of chaos and confusion such as Seth.

But how was a male principle in solitary splendour going to give birth to his progeny? Here the ingenuity of the Heliopolitan theologians was bound-less. Two accounts evolved of how the life-giving essence in Atum passed from his body to produce a god and goddess. Utterance 527 of the *Pyramid Texts* makes the unequivocal statement that Atum masturbated in Heliopolis: 'Taking his phallus in his grip and ejaculating through it to give birth to the twins Shu and Tefnut'. This direct imagery only makes sense if we remember that Atum possessed inside himself the prototype of every cosmic power and divine being. Otherwise, the word-picture of an orgasm by an ithyphallic sun god becomes a scurrilous caricature instead of an evocation of a sublime and mysterious act of creation.

In Utterance 600, however, the priests offer another explanation for the birth of Atum's children, relying on the assonance of words with similar consonantal skeletons. Punning was a useful tool of instruction in ancient Egypt, as shown by one example from a British Museum papyrus concerned with the interpretation of dreams: seeing a 'large cat' in a dream meant a 'bumper harvest' because the two phrases contained phonemes, or syllables, that were quite similar. So while not denying that the Egyptian sense of humour was pervasive and is all too often overlooked, we ought to regard the puns in the creation myths as attempts to convey intellectual concepts and not to elicit laughter at verbal dexterity – or, of course, groans at excruciating facetiousness. Atum is addressed as the god who 'spluttered out Shu and spat up Tefnut'. Shu is the mucus of Atum in as much as his name – from a root meaning 'void' or 'empty', an apt notion for the air god – is not too dissimilar to the word whose consonantal value is *yshsh* (no vowels are written in hieroglyphs) and which means 'sneeze' or 'splutter'. In the case of Tefnut, whose name eludes precise interpretation and is sometimes guessed to mean 'dew' or 'moisture in the air', the first two consonants of her name form the word *tf*, translated as 'spit'. Extracts from the Papyrus Bremner-Rhind bring together the salient points surrounding the procreative act of the Monad:

All manifestations came into being after I developed ... no sky existed no earth existed ... I created on my own every being ... my fist became my spouse ... I copulated with my hand ... I sneezed out Shu ... I spat out Tefnut ... Next Shu and Tefnut produced Geb and Nut ... Geb and Nut then gave birth to Osiris ... Seth, Isis and Nephthys ... ultimately they produced the population of this land.

The deities named here form the *Pesdjet* of Heliopolis, a group of nine gods and goddesses for which the Greek term *Ennead* is frequently used. Obviously the nine deities can be restricted to the genealogy devised at Heliopolis, but the notion of a coterie of gods and goddesses was transferable; the Temple of Abydos had an Ennead of seven deities while there were fifteen members of the Ennead in the Karnak temple. Probably because signs grouped in threes in Egyptian hieroglyphs conveyed the idea of an indeterminate plural, the concept of nine gods and goddesses indicates a plural of plurals, sufficient to cover a pantheon of any number of deities in any temple.

The first deities Atum created, Shu and Tefnut, could be represented as lions, as, for example, on the ivory headrest of Tutankhamun. In vignettes from the *Book of the Dead* Shu, wearing the ostrich plume which is in fact the hieroglyph for his name, raises his arms to support the body of the sky goddess Nut arched over her consort, the earth god Geb. Shu's role in the Heliopolitan cosmogony seems suppressed, no doubt because he had a strong solar streak in his nature that could not be allowed to approximate to the sun god *par excellence*. He encompassed the concept of air permeated by the rays of the sun – a notion used by the pharaoh Akhenaten in the earlier didactic name of the Aten, paramount sun god for less than two decades in the fourteenth century BC: 'Live Re-Horakhty rejoicing on the horizon – in his name as Shu who is in the Aten [i.e. sun disc]'.

Lioness-headed Tefnut escapes definitive categorisation. Her association with moisture or dew is attested in the *Pyramid Texts*, where there is also a passage suggesting that she is the atmosphere of the underworld. Perhaps the emphasis should be placed on her automatic access to the sun god, since as his daughter she becomes equated with his all-powerful solar eye.

The Heliopolitan view of the cosmos: the sky goddess Nut arches her body over her supine consort the earth god Geb from whom she is separated by the air god Shu, c. 1300 BC.

By natural processes Shu and Tefnut gave birth to Geb and Nut. Egyptians viewed the earth as a male principle and the sky female, in contrast to Indo-European mythology. Geb, the earth god, personified the land of Egypt and through him the link was established with the throne of the reigning pharaoh. The sky goddess Nut became one of the most represented deities from the elder Ennead. Her body is stretched across Geb but, after giving birth to four children, she is separated from him by Shu in accordance with the directive of Atum. Beyond her is Nu and non-existence. The ornate paintings of her in the sarcophagus hall of the tomb of Ramesses VI (1156–1148 BC) in the Valley of the Kings stress her importance – here the sun god journeys across the firmament along the underside of Nut's arched body; on reaching the western horizon at the end of the allotted twelve hours of day, the sun god is swallowed by the sky goddess; he traverses the inside length of her body during the hours of night, and at dawn Nut gives birth to the sun god on the eastern horizon amidst a display of redness that is the blood of parturition.

At this point in the genealogy, the priests of Heliopolis evolved a clever transition that incorporated the Osiris cycle of myths into the solar corpus. It lies in the fact that Nut bore Geb four children – Osiris, Isis, Seth and Nephthys. This created a connection between the elder cosmic deities of the Ennead and the political world. It also subordinated the upstart god Osiris, not attestable epigraphically or archaeologically before Dynasty V (2465–2323 BC), to the position of great-grandson of the sun god, thereby emphasising the impressive antiquity of the Monad. The legend of Osiris will be considered later but it is worth noting here that in completing the Ennead of Heliopolis the four offspring of Nut and Geb represent the perpetual cycle of life and death in the universe following Atum's act of creation. The Osiris cycle conforms to the dualism of the cosmic order established by the sun god and a balance is struck between the opposing principles of totality: Osiris *completes* a legitimate reign in Egypt; Seth *destroys* the lawful possessor of the throne of Geb. But more later.

The theogony of Heliopolis

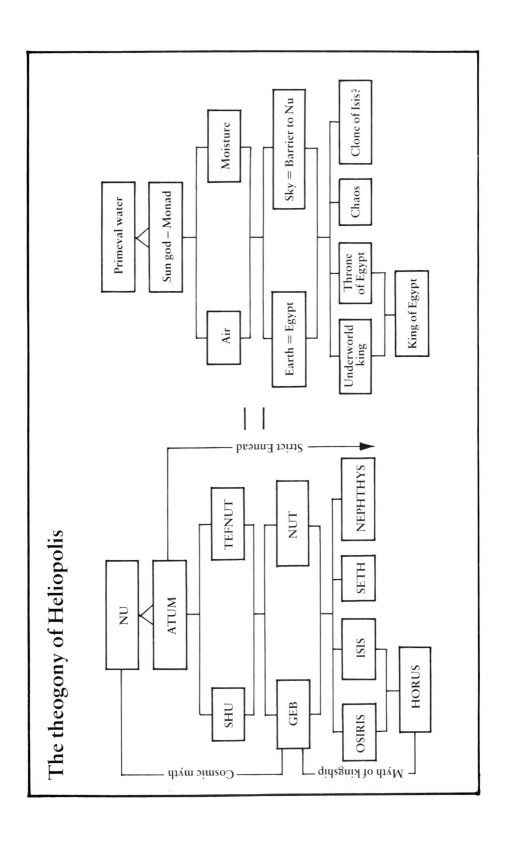

The imagery of the lotus flower seems to have been employed by the priests of Heliopolis to help explain the birth of the sun god Atum. Out of Nu emerged a lotus, together with the primeval mound, from which the sun god, still self-developed, rose as a child. The lotus itself was later identified with the god Nefertum (worshipped at Memphis); as a result there are spells in the *Book of the Dead* to transform the deceased into Nefertum because he is 'the lotus at the nose of the sun god'. In Cairo Museum the most beautiful portrayal of this concept can be found in the painted wooden lotus flower with the head of the child sun god emerging. It was found in the Valley of the Kings and is an iconographical identification of Tutankhamun with the newly-born sun god.

Before concluding the creation myth of Heliopolis we ought to mention the role of the Phoenix, the symbolism of the lotus and the coalescence of Atum with other manifestations of the sun god. The Phoenix, which the Greek writer Herodotus heard about in Egypt in the fifth century BC but did not see except in pictures on mythological papyri or wall carvings, originally took the form of a yellow wagtail but changed to a heron with long head plumes. In hieroglyphs it was called the *Benu*, the etymology of which means to 'rise in brilliance'. Self-evolved, the Benu became the symbol of the birth of the sun god. This is stated in Utterance 600 of the *Pyramid Texts* in an invocation to Atum: '... you rose up, as the Benben, in the Mansion of the Benu in Heliopolis'.

Herodotus was far from convinced about the existence of the Phoenix but related the story the priests had told him. The Herodotean Phoenix is a bird like an eagle, sporting gold and red plumage. On the death of its parent every five hundred years it flies from the Arabian peninsula to Egypt. It carries the body of its dead parent embalmed in an egg of myrrh and buries it in the Temple of the Sun God. The differences between the Phoenix of Herodotus and other classical authors, and the Benu of the ancient Egyptian sources are serious enough to make us question if the two birds are in any way related. However, Herodotus may have been confused by the evidence given to him. The bird he saw in pictures was certainly not the Benu, either in the shape he describes or in its gorgeous colouring; it was probably the Egyptian vulture or the Horus falcon. The mention of incense adds an authentic flavour, since it was highly valued in Egyptian temple ritual. The embalming myrrh of Herodotus' description could feasibly have been used in Heliopolis at this period in Egyptian civilisation, having come from the kingdoms of southern Arabia via the Red Sea trade routes.

For the rest, we ought not to forget that no-one knows the position of Herodotus' informants in the priestly hierarchy – upper echelons experienced in Heliopolitan theology or novices still learning. Indeed, some explanations of the Benu might have defeated the translators, especially since there are no records of Herodotus' time to inform us of any of the complexities of this bird that might have arisen during the two millennia following its first attestation in the *Pyramid Texts*. For example, we know that the Benu

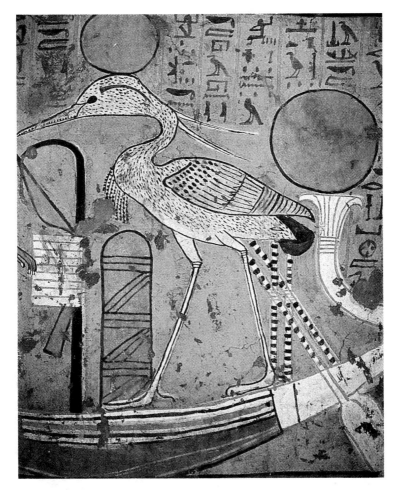

The Benu bird, or phoenix, manifestation of the sun god creator of Heliopolis.
Tomb of Arinefer at Deir el-Medina, Western Thebes, c. 1300 BC.

was incorporated in funerary rituals and had here come to play a role in ensuring the resurrection of the deceased in the underworld. The strongest point of contact between the Benu and the Phoenix is the connection that both have with the Temple of the Sun at Heliopolis.

Finally, the inner complexity of the Monad could project other manifestations. The coalescence of Atum with three aspects of the sun already existed by the time the *Pyramid Texts* were being inscribed. 'Re' is a basic word for sun indicating its physical presence in the sky and also the name of the sun god 'shining in his disk'; Khepri is the image of the sun propelled by a scarab beetle, an analogy taken from nature; Harakhti is the hawk soaring on the horizon, far off and distant as the sun itself. The names combine: for example, Re-Atum or Re-Harakhti. However, the essence of the myth of Heliopolis is not confused by this multiplicity of forms, each of which is an attempt to capture in a name an aspect of the sun god creator.

Ptah of Memphis

Ptah, 'south of his wall', was the god of Memphis, the ancient political capital of Egypt. In fact, in the New Kingdom (1550–1070 BC) his temple there, *Hewet-ka-Ptah* (Mansion of the spirit of Ptah), gave the name for the whole region and is ultimately the origin, via Greek, of the word Egypt itself. The ruins of Memphis today – for tourists mainly a calcite sphinx of Amenhotep II and a colossal statue of Ramesses II – offer little indication of the flourishing cosmopolitan city it once was. But leaving aside whatever splendid now-vanished monuments adorned the capital, Memphis demands our attention as the guardian of an intellectual tradition of cosmogony devised to assert the role of Ptah as most ancient and pre-eminent of gods. For it was here that the priests of Ptah formulated the metaphysical synthesis of creation preserved on the previously mentioned Shabaka Stone originally set up in their temple.

Before describing the contents of the Shabaka Stone, a word or two about Ptah as a creator god might be helpful. In the *Coffin Texts* and documents of the Ramesside era there are references to Ptah as being responsible for fashioning gods and the sun and for the ripening of vegetation. But even earlier in the Old Kingdom, Ptah's nature as a supreme artisan was fully developed and his High Priest at Memphis was called 'Greatest of the controllers of craftsmen'. From the reign of Ramesses II (1290–1224 BC) we find that the god Ptah coalesces with the deity Ta-tenen. The name Ta-tenen means 'the land which has become distinguishable', in other words, distinguishable from the primeval waters. Thus Ta-tenen risen from Nu can be equated with the primeval mound imagery already described. Now we can look at the Memphite account of creation beginning in column 53 of the Shabaka Stone.

Ptah gave life to the other gods (including Atum of Heliopolis) by means of his heart and his tongue. The conception of thought in the heart and the speech of the tongue determine the action of every limb. Ptah's presence is universal in the heart and mouths of 'all gods, all people, all cattle, all creeping things that live'. Ptah is superior to Atum, who brought his Ennead into being 'by his semen and his fingers'. The Ennead of Ptah is the teeth and lips in his mouth, so that by pronouncing the identity of everything the authority of his utterance was such that all creation came into being. Whatever the eyes see, the ears hear and the nose breathes goes straight to the heart, and the conclusion reached by the heart is then spoken by the tongue. This is how Ptah commanded all the gods into existence and how he became Ta-tenen, 'from whom all life emerged'. Having managed the birth of the gods, Ptah created for them cities, sanctuaries, shrines and perpetual offerings.

From this myth Ptah is seen to be an intellectual principle of creation amalgamated with the physical image of Ta-tenen as the primeval mound. It is a complete synthesis of mind and the material world. Known as the 'logos doctrine', there is a resounding echo of this impressive philosophical approach to the cosmos formulated by the priests of Memphis in the following passage from the New Testament:

> In the beginning was the Word and the Word was with God
> and the Word was God.
> The same was in the beginning with God.
> All things were made by Him; and without Him was not
> anything made that was made.
> In Him was life; and the life was the light of men.
> (St John's Gospel, Chapter 1, Verses 1–4)

This similarity of thought has received much attention. What has never been emphasised, however, is the small but mind-destroying step from his recognition of a possible creator-intelligence (eloquently propounded both by the priests of Memphis and St John) to the dogma of predestiny. The perfidious 'bridge' is the argument that since the supreme deity is both artisan of the human race and commander of order in the universe, his words have consequently planned all future events. Such a subservient acceptance of the idea of a pre-ordained course for the human race can be found in the verses of a poet quoted by Scheherazade:

> Go on your way and be comforted,
> Child of the Faithful;
> He who has moulded the world in His hands
> Holds it and us in His hands forever.
> What He has written you cannot alter,
> What He has not written never shall be ...
> Walk on light-hearted, caring and carrying nothing
> Leaving all to Him;
> Fear not what man may do, grieve not at sorrow,
> Especially plan not, for He has planned all things ...
> (*The Arabian Nights*, translated by Powys Mathers)

The priests of Memphis had argued and speculated in order to evolve the advanced principles of the logos doctrine. At times there must have been heated questioning of the nature of Ptah. But from this positive process emerged the Memphite cosmogony inscribed on the Shabaka Stone. Had a stultifying climate of unnegotiable religious tenets existed in pharaonic Egypt, it would have suppressed the initiatives of the priests of Ptah to grapple with what Omar Khayyam in Fitzgerald's *Rubaiyat* called the 'quarrel of the universe'.

The Ogdoad of Hermopolis

El-Ashmunein is a site in Middle Egypt that was once a prosperous city boasting an impressive temple built in honour of the god Djeheuty, better known by his Greek name of Thoth. The ruins are vast but overgrown and to unravel them demands full concentration, even for specialists. Although several archaeological expeditions, including the intensive British Museum excavations of the 1980s, have extended our knowledge about different developments on this site, most visitors to el-Ashmunein today will only be able to explore the huge Christian basilica constructed from re-used Roman columns and masonry. Because the region was the major cult centre of Thoth, god of wisdom and transmitter of the knowledge of hieroglyphs to the ancient Egyptians, the Greeks (who equated Thoth with their Hermes) referred to it as Hermopolis. In the Egyptian language, Hermopolis is called Khemnu, from which the modern Arabic name of el-Ashmunein ultimately derives, via Coptic. Khemnu means 'Eight Town' and was home to the eight primordial deities commonly known as the *Ogdoad* (a group of eight).

The myth of creation involving the Ogdoad is almost scientific in its concern with the physical composition of primeval matter. The original cosmic substance is seen as more complex than Nu, although Nu is counted among the mythical beings that it comprises. Admittedly the cosmology of Hermopolis lacks the imagery that surrounds the myth of the sun god of Heliopolis and the precision of the Memphite theology, but its scant statements probably result from the almost utter destruction or 'unexcavation' of inscribed pharaonic material at the site of el-Ashmunein. In fact, most evidence about the Ogdoad is drawn from Theban monuments pieced together in 1929 by the German Egyptologist Kurt Sethe in a masterly survey called 'Amun und die acht urgotter von Hermopolis'.

The number of either gods or goddesses in the Hermopolitan myth is far from fortuitous. We can see that four was regarded as the concept of a balanced totality: the Egyptians recognised four cardinal points, the Heliopolis myth gives the goddess Nut four children and the viscera extracted during embalming are protected by the four 'sons of Horus' with four goddesses guarding them in turn. Consequently the concept of eight is totality intensified – according to Spell 76 of the *Coffin Texts*, the god Shu created eight 'infinite beings' to help support the body of the sky goddess.

The eight of Hermopolis (structured as four couples) were personified entities within the primeval matter, with the gods envisaged as frogs and the goddesses as snakes. In the succinct phraseology of Henri Frankfort in his thought-provoking *Kingship and the Gods*, '. . . chaos had been conceptualised in eight weird creatures fit to inhabit the primeval slime'. The names of these eight deities survive, but it is difficult in some cases to conjure the exact mental image which ancient Egyptians would have seen. The following table gives the basic notion of each couple but ignores any divergence of concept which may have existed between the male and female principle:

Gods (frogs)	Goddesses (snakes)	Concept
Nu	Naunet	primeval waters
Heh	Hauhet	flood force
Kek	Kauket	darkness
Amun	Amaunet	concealed dynamism

In the case of Heh, philological evidence convincingly shows that the conventional translation of 'infinity' confuses two distinct words with similar consonantal stems.

At some point these entities who comprised the primordial substance interacted explosively and snapped whatever balanced tensions had contained their elemental powers. The formulators of the Hermopolitan cosmogony were convinced that the Ogdoad predated the Ennead of Heliopolis and were responsible for the origin of the sun. Accordingly, from the burst of energy released within the churned-up primal matter, the primeval mound was thrust clear. Its location later became Hermopolis, but its original emergence was described as the Isle of Flame because the sun god was born on it and the cosmos witnessed the fiery glow of the first sunrise. It was the primacy of the Ogdoad in this cataclysmic event that seems to have been paramount in the Hermopolis myth. In Egyptian terms, the Ogdoad are 'the fathers and the mothers who came into being at the start, who gave birth to the sun and who created Atum'. Events then develop in the newly created universe, but three pairs of the Ogdoad take no further interest and stay immune and immutable in the vortex. Amun and Amaunet, however, throw in their lot with the new order, and so desert Hermopolis for Thebes.

Finally, a tomb at Tuna el-Gebel, the desert necropolis for el-Ashmunein, adds an intriguing complication to the creation myth. Constructed in the style of a miniature temple shortly after the conquest of Egypt by Alexander the Great in 332 BC, it belonged to Petosiris, High Priest of Thoth at Hermopolis. He was also priest of the Ogdoad, but their withdrawal from the Hermopolitan scene after the Isle of Flame episode of the cosmogony

The ibis-headed god Thoth, head of the Ogdoad of creator deities of Hermopolis, in his role of divine scribe at the judgement of the dead. Before him is the Devourer of Evil Hearts and Osiris god of the underworld. Tomb of Petosiris at El-Mazauwaka, Dakhla Oasis. Hellenistic period.

meant that Thoth had taken the role of 'Lord of Khemnu'. Petosiris in his autobiographical inscriptions draws attention to the restorations he made to the temple complex at Hermopolis, severely damaged during the turmoil of the second Persian domination of Egypt in 343 BC. He revitalised the temple rituals, drew up a new rota for the priests and improved their promotion prospects. He conducted the foundation ceremony for a limestone temple to the sun god Re, who is referred to as the 'child in the Isle of Flame'. That conforms to the Hermopolitan myth, but now a new symbol of creation comes to the forefront. Petosiris describes how he built an enclosure around an area of the temple which had been vandalised by hooligans. He calls it the 'birthplace of every god' and states that there was outrage throughout Egypt at the damage. The reason for this outrage was that the relics of the cosmic egg from which the sun god broke out were buried there. Therefore, a new image of the sun god emerging from an egg had been introduced at Hermopolis. Possibly this scenario is an intrusion into the original myth, evolving around Thoth, who flew carrying the cosmic egg to the primeval mound at Khemnu for the birth of the sun god.

Amun the transcendent creator

During the New Kingdom Theban priests reached the heights of eloquence in hymns to the god Amun that extolled his uniqueness as creator. Like the analysis of the nature of the sun god Aten inscribed in the tomb of Ay at el-Amarna, these paeons, particularly the stanzas of Papyrus Leiden I 350, aimed to demonstrate that all elements of the physical universe were manifestations of a lone demiurge. There is a conflation of all notions of creation into the personality of Amun, a synthesis which emphasises how Amun transcends all other deities in his being 'beyond the sky and deeper than the underworld'. Time and again the Egyptian poet-priests tried to interpret Amun's inexplicability. His mystery is contained in his name – since his essence is imperceptible, he cannot be called by any term that hints at his inner nature, and so the name Amun has the underlying notion of 'hidden-ness' and probably best translates as 'the one who conceals himself'. His identity is so secret that no other god knows his true name. Amun – to venture a touch of lese-majesty – is the ultimate godfather, whose associates never know the extent of his involvements so that their safest policy is *omerta* (the Sicilian mafia code of silence). In the words of the Leiden hymn, Amun is 'too great to inquire into and too powerful to know'; the penalty for trying to get illicit information on his identity is expressly stated as instantaneous death.

Amun is synonymous with the growth of Thebes as a major religious capital. His prominence in that region is already attested in the Middle Kingdom, particularly as a god with procreative powers similar to the ancient ithyphallic deity Min, the primeval god of Coptos. His epithet to describe this possession of unfailing fertility is 'Bull of his mother', and the finest iconography of Amun in this character can be found on the peripteral chapel

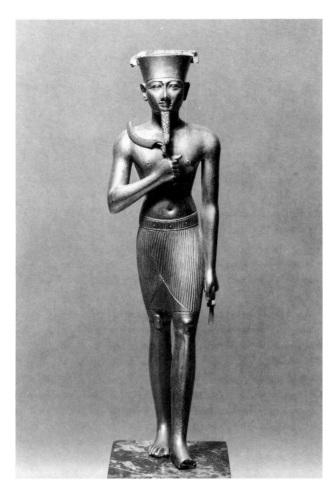

Gold statuette of the god Amun, transcendent creator and solar deity, holding the 'ankh' sign of life in one hand and the scimitar, symbol of power and foreign conquest, in the other.

of Senwosret I (1971–1926 BC) reconstructed in the open air museum at Karnak temple. It was, however, in the five centuries of the New Kingdom that Amun became undisputed head of the Egyptian pantheon (except for an eclipse of two decades when the 'sun disk' of the pharaoh Akhenaten was promoted to paramount god). Amun as universal ruler in his title of 'Lord of the thrones of the Two Lands' and 'King of the Gods' had such impressive temples built for him at Thebes that rumours of Thebes' splendour spread beyond the frontiers of Egypt into the world of composers of Greek epic poetry, as in Achilles' comments on Agamemnon:

I hate his gifts.
Not if he gave me ten times as much, and twenty times over as he possessed now, not if more should come to him from elsewhere ... all that is brought in to Thebes of Egypt, where the greatest possessions live up in the houses, Thebes of the hundred gates, where through each of the gates two hundred fighting men came forth to war with horses and chariots ... not even so would Agamemnon have his way with my spirit until he had made good to me all this heartrending insolence.
(from Homer's *Iliad*, Book IX, translated by Richmond Lattimore)

There were shrines to him, of course, elsewhere in Egypt and in the period following the New Kingdom the monarchs of Dynasties XXI–XXII (*c.* 1070–715 BC) redeployed colossal monuments from the reign of Ramesses II to build a huge temple to Amun, the northern equivalent of Karnak, at Tanis in the Delta. But it is to the columned halls, obelisks, colossal statues, wall-reliefs and hieroglyphic inscriptions of the Theban temples that we look to gain the true impression of Amun's superiority. Thebes was naturally thought of as the location of the emergence of the primeval mound at the beginning of time. It was the supreme 'city' and all other towns in Egypt could only try to imitate it and would only achieve pale reflections.

In the Hermopolitan creation myth, Amun is one of the elemental forces of the Ogdoad. But as the unique deity of the Theban theology he is transcendental, above creation and pre-existing the joint efforts of the Ogdoad to bring about the primeval mound. The Theban intellectuals must have struggled long and hard to resolve this problem. Amun as 'he who fashioned himself' generated himself into existence before all other matter existed. Without specific details of this mysterious event, the atmosphere of the occasion is evoked by the image of his 'fluid' becoming welded together with his body to form a cosmic egg. Once emerged, Amun forms the primeval matter – the elements of the Ogdoad of which he himself is a part. In this respect he becomes the 'First one who gave birth to the First ones'. But the universe was dark, silent and motionless. It seems that Amun was the creative burst of energy that stirred the Ogdoad into action. Kurt Sethe in his monograph interpreted Amun's role as similar to the 'Spirit of God' in Genesis that 'moved upon the face of the waters' – in other words, Amun was a stimulating breeze across primeval matter, stirring it into a vortex out of which the primordial mound would emerge. This is a tempting suggestion and the notion of wind is in keeping with Amun's invisibility. The Leiden hymn gives another rather amusing image of Amun initiating the activity of creation. The setting is the deadly quiet cosmos across which suddenly booms the voice of the 'Great Honker', not surprisingly 'opening every eye' and causing commotion in the cosmos. Amun in the form of this primeval goose set the whole process of creation in motion with his piercing screech.

The Theban theologians extensively develop the idea that all seemingly important deities are merely projections of Amun. Hence he does not stay in oblivion with the post-creation Ogdoad but becomes Ta-tenen, the primordial mound. He develops as the sun god, distant in the sky, continually rejuvenating in the cycle of sunset/sunrise. Therefore, his name on monuments as Amun-Re is legion. The Ennead of Heliopolis is a manifestation of Amun. In fact, every god is a projected image of Amun, and three gods in particular form a unity that is 'Amun': Re is his face, Ptah his body, and Amun his hidden identity.

As a postscript we can mention an aspect of Amun as a primeval deity that was probably restricted to the Theban region. If the creator god and assimilator of other deities described in the Leiden hymn proved to be too philosophical and intangible for some minds, then the Theban priests could provide a very concrete image of Amun as a primordial being. On the west bank of Thebes there is a site called Medinet Habu, much visited for its massive mortuary temple of the pharaoh Ramesses III (1194–1163 BC). Within its boundary walls is another temple lying to the north of the western fortified gate. Its construction in its present form dates from Dynasty XVIII with the joint reigns of Hatshepsut and Tuthmosis III (beginning about 1479 BC) through to the Graeco-Roman occupation into the reign of Antoninus Pius (AD 138–161). The statue of Amun of Karnak would regularly be brought to this sanctuary with the sole purpose of greeting his ancestor, a primeval form of himself imagined as a snake. The snake was described as 'Kem-atef' or 'The one who has completed his moment'. This could be a reference to the darting swiftness of a snake and with it an inherent analogy of the burst of energy from Amun at the creation. It could also be suggestive of the snake shedding its skin and hence symbolic of the procreative power of Amun and the continual cycle of renewal of life. The Greek writer Plutarch (c. AD 40–120) described the snake as 'Kneph', mentioning that the inhabitants of Thebes worshipped it to the exclusion of all other gods. In that statement Plutarch was decidedly wrong, but his epithets for the snake are drawn from traditions that accurately reflected this ancestral form of Amun as 'unbegotten and immortal'.

Khnum and the Theban theogony

The god Khnum, a ram-headed god of the cataract region of the Nile, introduces a new emphasis in creation myths in that his main concern is with the making of humans. He is thought to have moulded the human form on a potter's wheel. Elsewhere, in the Heliopolitan and Hermopolitan myths

The creator god Khnum in his manifestation as a ram. At his temple at Esna the myth explained how Khnum created mankind on the potter's wheel. Late Period.

for example, the human race is all but ignored in favour of cosmic issues. But in the myth of Khnum there is a progressive link between the gods and the people of the world. The ram, Khnum's sacred creature, is a symbol of procreativity in the natural world. At Aswan in the Nile cataract, Khnum controlled the caverns of Hapy, the god of the inundation. Before the modern irrigation projects at Aswan, culminating in the High Dam (which destroyed the natural regime of the Nile), the River would flood annually. The water covered the fields and on receding left a mantle of the rich silt it had carried with it from the Sudan. On the fertile mud Egyptian farmers grew barley and emmer-wheat and harvests normally resulted in a surplus of grain. So the inundation meant prosperity, and Khnum its controller was seen as a benefactor to the people of Egypt. A ruined sanctuary of Khnum as 'lord of the cataract' sprawls over the southern end of the island of Elephantine at Aswan.

In the temple of Esna in Upper Egypt Khnum was celebrated as the creator of all people. The town of Esna today, apart from occasional Islamic architecture of merit, is a squalid urban cluster. The main street leading to the temple from the River is just north of the ancient ceremonial approach, now buried deep below the modern town. All that survives of Khnum's temple is the hypostyle hall predominantly Roman in date. The inscriptions on the columns and walls are in the deliberately complex form of the hieroglyphic script favoured by the priest-scribes of the Graeco-Roman era. Nevertheless, it is from the calender liturgies and hymns carved at Esna that we derive the clearest understanding of Khnum as creator and god of the potter's wheel.

Khnum's actions in moulding the human body on the wheel are explicitly stated and survive as a detailed anatomical record. He orientated the blood-stream to flow over the bones and attached the skin to the body's frame. He installed a respiratory system in the body, vertebrae to support it and an apparatus for digestion. In keeping with his procreative responsibilities he designed the sexual organs to allow maximum comfort without loss of efficiency during intercourse. He supervised conception in the womb and initiated the stages of labour. Chanted at the Festival of the Potter's Wheel, the above hymn must have sounded like a metrical medical manual. Other descriptions emphasise that Khnum's moulding on the wheel is a continual process and not just restricted to Egyptians but to those who speak foreign languages as well. He is thus a universal creator who formed gods and people, animals, birds, fish and reptiles.

It has been suggested that the idea of Khnum moulding a human being on the potter's wheel, which goes far back in Egypt in reliefs and inscriptions of the Temple of Esna, could have influenced the traditions that the Greek poet Hesiod (c. 700 BC) drew upon for the making of Pandora which he describes both in his *Theogony* and *Works and Days*. There Zeus instructed Hephaistos to mould a woman, Pandora, out of clay, who would bring mankind limitless miseries. But it is quite probable that the Hesiodic concept of Pandora is an independent tradition – certainly the malicious intentions of Zeus are far from the spirit of the philanthropic Khnum. There are also later Middle Eastern surmises upon the idea of the creation of people on the potter's wheel. For instance, Omar Khayyam, in Fitzgerald's *Rubaiyat*, contains a scene in a potter's shop in Iran, probably Naishapur, around AD 1200. The 'clay population' converse with one another, each with a human angst: 'Then said another – "Surely not in vain my substance from the common earth was ta'en that He who subtly wrought me into shape should stamp me back to common earth again"'.

We can now move from the general encomium at Esna about Khnum's importance in human life to an interesting commission that the god Amun entrusted to him at Thebes. The episode is known as the Theban theogony. This describes the 'marriage' (actually a brief sexual encounter) between the god Amun and the great royal wife. There are in fact two examples of the theogony in Theban temples: one relating to the birth of Queen Hatshepsut at Deir el-Bahri and the other, which we will follow through here, concerning the pharaoh Amenhotep III (1391–1353 BC).

The procreative form of Amun, with his self-renewing energy conjured up by the epithet 'Ka-mutef' or 'Bull of his mother', predominates in the Temple of Luxor on the east bank at Thebes. Near to the sanctuary, which in its present form bears the cartouches of Alexander the Great, Amenhotep III gave orders for the construction of an apartment where the results of Amun's unfailing sexual powers could be unfurled in a series of reliefs that enhanced the monarch's own divinity. The pharaoh was called from the Pyramid era onwards (in particular from *c.* 2500 BC) the 'Son of the sun god' – this was in addition to being the early manifestation of the god Horus. The sandstone reliefs at Luxor, now horrendously pitted, define this kinship to the creator god, the status now held by Amun, in a 'royal wedding' documentary.

From the hieroglyphs it is clear that Amun, 'the one who conceals himself', has taken on the guise of the pharaoh Tuthmosis IV (1401–1391 BC) in order to make the earthly projection of himself a reassuring figure for the queen involved. However, the depictions show Amun in his traditional iconography as state god: anthropomorphic, beard of divinity with the curled tip and a crown of two high plumes. The first scene chronologically shows Queen Mut-em-wiya, great royal wife of Tuthmosis IV, seated opposite Amun on a long couch which can also be read as the hieroglyph for sky. So we can assume that the scenario is symbolically Amun's place in the heavens far removed from the palace bedroom. The sexual union is discreetly represented – both Mut-em-wiya and Amun are clothed in their linen garments but their legs are in a formalised entanglement; Amun's right hand extends the 'ankh', sign of life, to the nose of Mut-em-wiya for her to breathe in its vitality. This is the moment of orgasm and of transmission of the god's semen into the queen. Supporting the sky-couch with their heads and holding the feet of the god and queen are the protective scorpion goddess Serket and the demiurge-goddess Neith.

The next scene brings Khnum onto the stage. Amun, holding his sceptre of dominion and the sign of life, approaches the ram-headed Khnum who carries similar regalia. Instructions are passed on to Khnum. Now Khnum comes into his own. He sits on a throne, his hands resting on the heads of the two child-beings he has just moulded, who stand on the stylised potter's wheel. One figure is the future King Amenhotep III, and the other represents the 'ka' or eternal life-force of the pharaoh. The goddess Hathor, in one aspect guardian of royalty, is seated by the wheel and holds up the 'ankh' sign to the two figures. Mystery then surrounds the method of implantation of these moulded beings into the womb of the queen by Khnum. We are then shown the birth of Amenhotep III. Queen Mut-em-wiya is seated on a cube-shaped chair in the centre of a gigantic couch guarded by lion-head terminals. Both her posture and her chair are stylisations of the real-life situation where women knelt over the 'brick of pregnancy' (representing the goddess Meskhenet) to give birth. Two midwives hold on to the arms of Mut-em-wiya, but unfortunately there is a large gash in the sandstone damaging details around the queen's abdomen. These surrounding reliefs, however, indicate that there has been a successful delivery of Amenhotep III and his 'ka'.

The Theban theogony is incapable of any interpretation suggesting that Amun is abusing his prerogative as supreme god in order to enjoy a one-night stand with the Queen of Egypt. Their union is a far cry from the indiscriminate lusts of certain Greek deities whom Lord Byron clearly had in mind when he wrote:

> What men call gallantry, and gods adultery,
> Is much more common when the climate's sultry.
> (Don Juan, *Canto* I:LXIII)

In Egypt for the god-pharaoh to be proclaimed as the offspring of the king of the gods constituted a propaganda myth aimed at 'hierarchising' the monarchs into second-in-command in the cosmos. The reputation of his predecessor was in no way tarnished. The queen was elevated – albeit momentarily – to consort of the supreme god in an intimacy beyond the reach of the pharaoh himself. The god Amun became manifest early on in a calculated liaison with Mut-em-wiya with the purpose of engendering a future regent to control Egypt in his name. To borrow phrases from W. B. Yeats' *Leda and the Swan* – the queen of Egypt in her lovemaking with the king of the gods could well have 'put on his knowledge and his power'. Furthermore, Amun's motivation in ensuring that the heir to the throne of Egypt would be totally unassailable, through an extraterrestrial input of DNA, creates a mood light-years away from the turbulent passion of the Greek god Zeus that led to the disasters of:

> The broken wall, the burning roof and tower
> and Agamemnon dead.

The myth of kingship

The legitimate succession of a pharaoh to the throne of Egypt was on the one hand a very practical affair, possibly involving a stabilising period of co-regency with the previous monarch, and on the other an event hallowed by mythological precedent. The basic dogma of the ruler-cult proclaimed that the pharaoh was the earthly manifestation of the sky god Horus. So the myth of the transmission of kingship from Osiris via the machinations of Isis to her son Horus is vital to understanding the status and power of the sovereign in ancient Egypt and shall be explained here.

The records from which it is possible to piece together the myth of kingship are varied in nature and date. In the case of Osiris as monarch of Egypt before his departure to become king of the underworld I have concentrated on the *Pyramid Texts*, spells on the coffins of courtiers in the Middle Kingdom and the stela of Amenmose in the Louvre Museum. Ancient Egyptian sources are noticeably reticent about the murder of Osiris and the usurpation of the throne by Seth, but there are intriguing references such as in the stela of Ikhernofret in Berlin Museum (no. 1204), and in a Ptolemaic papyrus (no. 3008 in Berlin Museum) concerned with the grief of Isis. I have used Papyrus Chester Beatty I, an extremely lively papyrus in the Dublin Museum as documentation for the violent, salacious and hilarious episodes of the struggle between Seth and Horus for the throne. The eventual vindication of Horus as the rightful ruler of Egypt draws upon the Shabaka Stone, the Middle Kingdom Ramesseum Dramatic Papyrus and the play concerning the annihilation of Seth inscribed on the wall of the ambulatory passage in Edfu Temple, dating to the Ptolemaic period. Finally, at the end of the myth as it is found in pharaonic sources, I have appended a brief synopsis of the account called 'Concerning Isis and Osiris' by the Greek author Plutarch (c. AD 40–120), where original Egyptian elements have been interwoven with Hellenistic concepts.

The murder of Osiris

From the creation myth devised by the priests of Heliopolis we can observe a clever link between the cosmic deities and the gods and goddesses who figure in the story of the transmission of kingship. Geb the earth god and Nut the sky goddess produced four children – Osiris, Isis, Seth and Nephthys. By this genealogy there is a descent from the sun god creator to the possessor of the throne of Egypt. Osiris was the firstborn of the offspring of Geb and Nut. His birthplace was near Memphis at Rosetau in the western desert necropolis. This spot was particularly apt for the birth of Osiris since his pre-eminent role is that of the god of the underworld and Rosetau, or 'Mouth of the passage-ways', is the symbolic entrance into Osiris' nether realm. An epithet, originally for a funerary deity at Abydos, which Osiris often carries is 'Khenta-mentiu', or 'Foremost of the Westerners', a title which similarly emphasises Osiris' status as ruler of those buried in the desert cemeteries whence their spirits hoped for access into the underworld.

As the eldest son of Geb and Nut, Osiris inherited the right to govern the land of Egypt. In the traditions of kingship preserved in the New Kingdom papyrus known as the Turin Royal Canon, Egypt in predynastic times was under the rule of a succession of gods – Ptah, Re, Shu, Geb, Osiris, Seth and Horus. (We have to ignore here its continuation with Thoth, Maet and the Followers of Horus.) Osiris' consort was his sister Isis, thus providing a divine prototype for marriage between full or half-brothers and sisters in the royal family. The prosperity of Egypt during his reign is conjured up in eloquent phraseology on the stela of Amenmose (c. 1400 BC during Dynasty XVIII) in the Louvre Museum. There, Osiris is described as commanding all resources and elements in a way that brings good fortune and abundance to the land. Through his power the waters of Nu are kept under control, favourable breezes blow from the north, plants flourish and all animal life follows a perfect pattern of procreation. Also Osiris receives immense respect from other gods and governs the system of stars in the sky. Of his cult centres throughout Egypt the mid-Delta sanctuary of Djedu (Busiris) and his Upper Egyptian temple at Abydos are paramount. His regalia consists of the crook and flail sceptres and tall plumed 'atef' crown described as 'sky-piercing'. So like many stories throughout history we begin with a benevolent and successful king and queen, Osiris and Isis, ruling in a golden age.

This idyllic scene is now shattered by the usurpation of the throne by Seth, Osiris' antagonist-brother. Tradition maintained that Seth ripped himself from the womb of Nut in Upper Egypt at Naqada where his major temple in the south was later erected. Violence and chaos became attributes of Seth but despite his 'bad press' in the myth of kingship we ought not to overlook the fact that occasions stand out when support for this god was strong. Certainly on present archaeological evidence Seth is a god of greater antiquity than Osiris, since we find the composite creature which represents him on the late predynastic macehead of King Scorpion, a ruler of Upper Egypt, in the Ashmolean Museum, Oxford. (At present no archaeological proof exists for Osiris before Dynasty V, c. 2465 BC.) The Seth animal has a slightly crescent-shaped proboscis and two upright projections from the top of its head and – if represented in complete quadrupedic form rather than just the head on an anthropomorphic body – it has an erect forked tail.

In the *Pyramid Texts* there are tantalising references to Osiris suffering a fatal attack from this creature. He is described as 'falling on his side' on

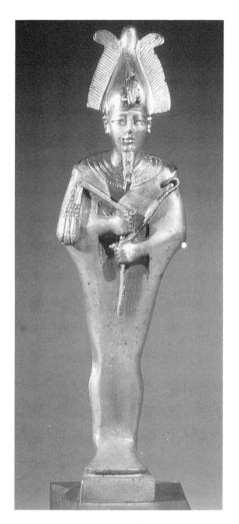 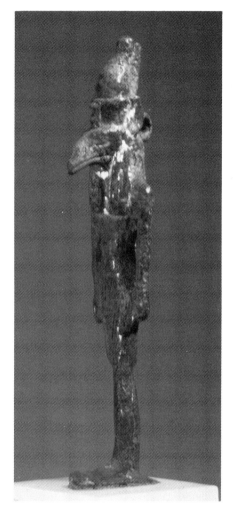

ABOVE LEFT *The god Osiris, who in the myth of kingship inherits the throne from Geb, is murdered by Seth and becomes ruler of the underworld. His distinctive 'atef' crown comprises ram-horns and ostrich feathers. Late-Period bronze.*

ABOVE RIGHT *Seth, god of chaotic forces and opponent of Osiris and Horus in the myth of kingship. Outside this myth, Seth was regarded as an ancient and prestigious deity. Here, above the head of his heraldic creature, he wears the Double Crown of a pharaoh. Late-Period bronze.*

the river bank at Nedyet in the district of Abydos. His murder is confirmed by the grief displayed in the weeping of Isis. The spells painted on the coffins of courtiers in the Middle Kingdom identify the murderer of Osiris unequivocally as Seth, and declare that he attacked Osiris in Gahesty and killed him by the river at Nedyet. These sparse details reflect the horror held by the Egyptians of the assassination of the monarch and violent transfer of power – it was a theme not to be developed or dwelt upon. It is interesting to note that historically there are relatively few instances of bloody *coups d'état* during the first two thousand years of dynastic Egypt. In fact there are several inscriptions that try to suppress the idea that Osiris was murdered – although subsequent events do not make sense without his death. An example is the hymn on the stela of Amenmose where Osiris is portrayed as invincible, a slayer of foes and crusher of conspirators, although a little later in the text Isis is searching for his body. Similarly the valuable inscription on the stela of Ikhernofret in Berlin Museum re-interprets the event into a victory-procession for the adherent of Osiris. This stela gives an insight into the rituals in honour of Osiris held at his major cult centre at Abydos: Ikhernofret was an official of King Senwosret III (1878–1841 BC) commissioned by the pharaoh to organise the annual festival of Osiris at Abydos and adorn the sacred image of the god with gold. During the ceremonies the statue of Osiris in the regalia of kingship, decked out with lapis lazuli, turquoise and gold, was carried on the 'Neshmet' boat. The ancient canine deity Wepwawet acted as the champion of Osiris during this procession. There follows the suppression of the assassination of Osiris: the 'Neshmet' boat is symbolically attacked but during the combat it is the foes of Osiris who are killed by the river at Nedyet. Illogically, the next stage of the ceremony is to conduct the funerary boat of Osiris to his tomb in the desert of Abydos at Peqer. Incidentally, this tomb was located towards the desert cliffs in the region called by the Arabs 'Umm el-Ga'ab' or 'Mother of Pots' from the vast quantity of pottery offered on the early dynastic royal monument that had become re-interpreted as the god's sepulchre.

With Osiris dead, Seth becomes ruler of Egypt, with his sister Nephthys as his consort. However, the sympathies of Nephthys are with her sister Isis who is distraught at the death of Osiris. Isis determines to use her immense magical powers to recover the body of Osiris and to resurrect it sufficiently to conceive a son to avenge the monstrous usurpation and murder. Tirelessly she and Nephthys roam Egypt lamenting Osiris until eventually his body is located at Abydos. Other cult centres claimed to be the resting place of Osiris' body – or parts of it – such as the Abaton on Biga Island just south of the First Cataract of the Nile at Aswan or Herakleopolis where the burial was held to be under the 'Naret-tree', but it is at Abydos that we find the fullest documentation of the next episode in the myth.

Therefore, let us go into the shrine of the god Sokar in the Temple of King Sety I (1306–1290 BC), at Abydos. This temple is renowned for the most exquisite reliefs to have survived in Egyptian art, primarily in the seven sanctuaries and in the suite of inner apartments dedicated to Osiris, Isis and Horus. The Sokar sanctuary has suffered severe damage but two representations give explicit visual indications of the impregnation of Isis with the seed of Osiris. In the inscription of Amenmose the goddess Isis discovers the body of Osiris, shades it with her wings (she can take the form of a kite) and creates the breath of life with her wings so that Osiris revives from death and impregnates her. Similarly on the walls of the Abydos temple this act of procreation involves the magic of Isis and her transformation into a sparrow hawk to receive the seed of Osiris. One representation shows Isis and (by anticipation) Horus at either end of the lion-headed bed of mummification. Osiris, whose putrefaction has been halted by the skills of Isis, raises one arm to his head which Isis is holding and grasps his phallus in the other hand to stimulate it into orgasm. The other depiction follows on from this act with Isis as the sparrow hawk pressing herself down upon the phallus of Osiris. Osiris' role in the myth of kingship in Egypt is now completed. He descends into Duat, the underworld, and reigns there as Lord of Eternity. In Egyptian religious thought it was not the earthly rule of Osiris that was significant but the miracle of his resurrection from death, offering the hope of a continuity of existence for everyone in the underworld where one of Osiris' titles proclaims him as 'ruler of the living'. As can be seen, the main protagonist has become the goddess Isis, the hieroglyphs of whose name contain the symbol of the throne.

The vengeance of Horus

The resulting child of Isis and Osiris is the hawk god Horus. His name means the 'Far-Above-One', derived from the imagery of the soaring of the hawk. Horus is a complex deity into whom have been amalgamated concepts not directly involved in the myth of kingship – the idea of the god as a vulnerable child or as the sky-falcon whose eyes are the sun and moon. However, all diverse elements were skilfully woven into a tapestry, the sum total of whose different emphases was the god Horus with whom the sovereign of Egypt identified.

The hawk Horus,
god of kingship.
Ptolemaic period bronze.

Horus was born in the North East Delta at Khemmis. For his own security against Seth, Isis hid Horus in the papyrus marshes. During his early years he is called Har-pa-khered or 'Horus the child', referred to by the Greeks as Harpokrates. He is vulnerable and dependent on the magic of the goddess Isis for protection (see the chapter *Isis 'Great in Magic'*). When he reaches his maturity as Har-wer or 'Horus the Elder' (Haroeris in Greek) he is ready to struggle for his rightful patrimony, the throne of Egypt, but as we shall see the goddess Isis is crucial still in helping him achieve this end.

Horus takes his claim to the kingship of Egypt to a tribunal of major gods presided over by the sun god Re of Heliopolis. He has chosen a propitious moment to submit his case – when Thoth, god of wisdom, is presenting the sun god with the 'Sacred Eye', symbolic of cosmic order, justice and kingship. The air god Shu urges the immediate approval of Horus' claim and Thoth adds that such a decision would be a 'million times right'. Isis in her excitement prepares the north wind to carry the good news to Osiris in the underworld. However, the gods have begun to act prematurely since Re intervenes to point out that their decision does not yet have his ratification. He deplores their insistence that Horus already possesses the royal name-ring (i.e. the cartouche in which the hieroglyphs spelling two of the five names of a monarch were written) and the White Crown of Upper Egypt. Seth suggests that he and Horus should go outside the courtroom and settle the matter by hand-to-hand combat. Thoth tries to restore some notion of the procedures of a law court and emphasises that Horus has a good case since he is the son of Osiris. The sun god, however, is not impressed and clearly prefers Seth 'great of strength'.

An impasse is reached and lasts eighty years. To try and break it, the gods eventually agree on sending a letter to the great creator goddess Neith. The letter is dispatched in the name of Re and is couched in deferential terms to the goddess, seeking her advice. In contrast an impatient and curt reply comes from Neith, stressing the clear-cut evidence in favour of Horus who should inherit the office of Osiris – otherwise 'the sky will crash down' at this offence against justice. Neith is also an astute judge since she realises that Seth must be given a consolation prize and urges Re to give him his two daughters Anat and Astarte as wives. These Middle Eastern goddesses had become incorporated in the Egyptian pantheon in the New Kingdom, as had the important Syrian gods Baal and Reshep. Since Seth has an affinity with foreign warrior gods the gift of these two goddesses is quite apt. The gods of the tribunal approve Neith's advice, except for Re. He finds the decision totally unacceptable and turns on Horus to abuse him. He accuses Horus of being a weakling, a youngster with halitosis and certainly not strong enough to wield authority. The tribunal of gods now becomes exasperated and a minor god called Baba has the audacity to tell Re 'Your shrine is empty' which is tantamount to saying that no one takes him seriously any more. Re now exhibits a remarkable sensitivity to this remark, abandoning the tribunal to go off to his pavilion and sulk. The situation is saved, however, by

Hathor, 'mistress of the southern sycamore', who is another daughter of Re and a goddess of love and joy. Hathor goes to Re's pavilion, stands in front of him and pulls up her dress to reveal her nakedness. For some reason this display provokes Re to laughter. He returns to the courtroom and tells Horus and Seth to submit their cases.

Seth, who is portrayed in this papyrus as a swaggerer and boaster, claims he deserves the throne of Egypt by virtue of his unassailable strength. Only he is competent to repel Apophis, the arch enemy of the sun god, on the journey through the underworld. This claim meets with approval since Apophis was a very real threat to the existence of the cosmos. But Thoth and Anhur (a warrior god originating near Abydos) question whether it is lawful to give an inheritance to the brother while the son is capable of taking it. A counter-claim argues that Seth as the elder of the two disputants deserves the office. (It is here that the papyrus refers to Horus and Seth as brothers, an independent tradition conflated into the 'uncle-nephew' account.) At this point Isis loses patience and intervenes on behalf of Horus, gaining the tribunal's sympathy. This infuriates Seth who threatens to kill one god a day with his 4500lb sceptre. He takes an oath in the name of Re to protest that he will not recognise any court in which Isis participates. Re removes the proceedings to an island, giving orders to the ferryman Nemty not to row across any women resembling Isis.

But this move underestimates the guile and magic of Isis. Disguised as an old crone carrying a bowl of flour and wearing a gold signet ring, Isis approaches Nemty. Her request is for the ferryman to row her across to the island so that she can give the flour for food to a hungry young herdsman who has been tending cattle for five days. Nemty informs her that he has received orders to ferry no women across to the island but has to admit that the old woman does not seem to be the goddess Isis. In a touch of realism which you might encounter in Egypt today, bargaining now begins over the price of the journey. Nemty is contemptuous of a cake which Isis offers and only agrees to ferry her across in exchange for the gold signet ring which he duly receives.

Once on the island Isis sees the gods having a break and eating bread. Uttering a spell to change herself into a beautiful young woman, she catches the eye of Seth who is immediately excited with desire. He comes over alone to Isis and introduces himself. Isis cleverly traps Seth into an admission of guilt – she pretends to be a herdsman's widow whose son is being threatened by a stranger with the confiscation of his father's cattle and eviction from his home. She implores Seth to act as her son's defender. Seth feels great indignation at the injustice she and her son are suffering. This is, of course, precisely what Isis had hoped for since by analogy it is the contest for the inheritance of Osiris. For her own safety she changes into a kite and flies onto an acacia, informing Seth that his verdict has condemned him. Amazingly, Seth bursts into tears and goes off to complain to Re about the trickery of Isis. Re has no option but to tell Seth that he has not been too bright in condemning himself. Seth now shows a vindictive streak and asks for Nemty the ferryman to be brought to the tribunal. Nemty is found guilty of disobedience and has his toes cut off as punishment. The court now moves to a mountain in the western desert. The tribunal awards the throne of Egypt to Horus but the execution of this decision is thwarted by the successful appeal of Seth to challenge Horus to a contest.

Thus begins a series of episodes aimed at discrediting Seth. The first is almost ridiculous in its concept. Seth challenges Horus that they should both change into hippopotami and submerge themselves under the water for three months. If either of them surfaces before this time then he will lose his claim to the throne. Horus agrees and they both plunge, as hippopotami, into the water. Isis suddenly becomes concerned that Seth intends to kill her son underwater and decides to eliminate him. She makes a copper harpoon and hurls it at the spot where they submerged. Her first throw misses the mark and strikes Horus. She conjures it out of him when he naturally complains. On her second attempt she makes a direct hit on Seth but when he pleads with her that there is a brother-sister blood bond between them she relents and conjures the harpoon out of his body.

The next sequence is quite bizarre. Horus emerges from the water in a rage at Isis for sparing the life of Seth. He cuts off her head and carries it with him into the desert mountains. Isis' body becomes a flint statue and remains headless. Re inquires of Thoth who the strange decapitated statue represents. Thoth tells Re the story of what has happened and Re promptly becomes angry and avows that Horus will be punished and gives orders for the desert to be searched. (At some point, not mentioned in the papyrus, Isis' head is restored.) Seth discovers Horus lying under a tree in an oasis of the western desert. He pounces on him and gouges out his eyes, burying them in the desert where they turn into lotus flowers. Naturally he assumes that this is the end of his adversary and on his return to Re denies ever having found Horus. However, Hathor comes across the distressed Horus and rubs his eyes with gazelle milk. Magically, they are perfectly healed. When Re is informed of events he finally loses his patience and summons Horus and Seth. He orders them to stop quarrelling as they are getting on everyone's nerves.

Seth, the supreme trickster, apparently accepts a reconciliation and invites Horus to a feast at his home. Later that night Seth makes a homosexual approach to Horus who, unbeknown to Seth, deflects the attack and with his hands between his thighs catches the semen of Seth. Horus informs Isis who is horrified when he holds out his hand with the semen in it. Obviously regarding her son's hand as polluted, she cuts it off and throws it into the marshes; her magic manufactures Horus a new hand. She then devises a ploy to make Seth's trickery rebound on himself. With scented unguent Isis arouses Horus' phallus and stores his semen in a jar. She goes into the garden and spreads the semen on the lettuces, Seth's favourite plants. Soon Seth comes and eats the very same lettuces. He then plans to make Horus a laughing-stock before the gods and proclaims in the court that he has homosexually dominated Horus which leads to the other gods expressing their contempt for Horus by spitting in front of him. In return Horus laughs and accuses Seth of telling lies, suggesting that their respective semen be summoned to discover its location. Thoth, with his arm on Horus, summons the semen of Seth to come forth, which it does, only not from Horus but from the marshwater. Holding Seth's arm, Thoth then summons Horus' semen which emerges as a gold sun disk from the head of Seth. By this scurrilous episode Seth is humiliated and Horus vindicated.

Still Seth refuses to admit defeat and suggests a ludicrous contest which cannot but seem a monument to misspent energy: the rivals must make ships of stone to race against each other. Horus craftily builds a ship of pinewood, coated with a limestone plaster to give it the appearance of stone. Seth sees it launched and then cuts off a mountain peak to shape a boat 138 cubits (70 m) long. Before the assembled gods Seth's boat sinks. In anger Seth turns into a hippopotamus and shatters Horus' boat. Horus seizes a weapon but is prevented by the gods from killing Seth. In sheer frustration Horus sails to the cult sanctuary of the goddess Neith at Sais and explains his incomprehension at how, with so many judgements in his favour, he still does not have his rightful inheritance.

Meanwhile, Thoth persuades Re to write a letter to Osiris in the underworld. In it Osiris is given a full royal title which eulogises his powers. Osiris' response to the question of the decision between Horus and Seth is to accentuate his own role in making the gods strong with emmer-wheat and barley and thereby not to defraud his son Horus. In pique Re replies that the gods would have had barley and emmer-wheat whether Osiris existed or not. Threats now come from the underworld: Osiris points out that he has at his command bloodthirsty agents who are in awe of no god or goddess and would willingly search out and bring back to him the heart of any wrongdoer. In addition the stars in the sky, the gods and mankind all descend into the Western Horizon and so into the realm of Osiris. On the sober reflection of these facts the tribunal of gods are now unanimous in vindicating Horus and establishing him upon the throne of his father. Seth suffers a final humiliation when, as Isis' prisoner, he is led before the gods to relinquish his claim to the throne of Egypt. Re, however, still feels a special regard for Seth and announces that Seth will accompany him in the sky and that his voice will be the thunder in the heavens.

The Edfu drama

As stressed in the account given in the papyrus Chester Beatty 1, the claim of Horus to the throne is vindicated but Seth is protected by Re, the sun god. If, however, we go to the major temple of Horus at Edfu in Upper Egypt, we are confronted with the same outcome for Horus but the treatment of Seth is totally destructive. At Edfu the tradition of the annihilation of

Seth was portrayed vividly in the form of a drama acted annually at the Festival of Victory. Both hieroglyphs and vignettes were used to encapsulate the essential features of the play. The temple in its present form dates to the Ptolemaic era but was built across more ancient structures on that site. Similarly, although the drama in its surviving form is dated to the reign of Ptolemy IX (*c.*110 BC), its origin is much earlier, probably with a prototype of New Kingdom date.

In the drama Seth is in the form of a hippopotamus and is shown in different scenes pierced by harpoons. The victors are the king and Horus urged on by Isis. Harpooning the hippopotamus is an ancient royal ritual which we find on cylinder seal impressions from the First Dynasty (*c.*3000–2770 BC). At Edfu, the scenes involve ten harpoons, each piercing a different part of the hippopotamus' anatomy. Certainly a model hippopotamus would have been manufactured for the Festival and have been the 'villain' of the show. In the vignettes the hippopotamus is shown diminutive in stature so that it could be contained and trapped if there was any magical animation from the wall. The viciousness and total destruction brought about by the spearing at the hands of Horus is conveyed both by vignette and hieroglyphs:

Harpoon	Part of Seth injured
First	Snout – nostrils severed
Second	Forehead
Third	Neck
Fourth	Back of head
Fifth	Ribs
Sixth	Vertebrae
Seventh	Testicles
Eighth	Haunches
Ninth	Legs
Tenth	Hocks

The symbol of the triumph of the god Horus is the depiction of him riding the back of the Seth-hippopotamus and spearing its head. Horus wears the Double Crown of Upper and Lower Egypt. Most noticeable is the aggression of Isis in the Edfu drama, since it is such a contrast to the Isis who exhibits compassion for her brother Seth in the papyrus of the struggle for the throne. At the dismemberment of the hippopotamus Isis urges the distribution of the limbs to various deities, with the bones going to cats and the fat to worms. In a final ritual a hippopotamus cake is solemnly sliced up and eaten – the ultimate annihilation of Seth.

The ritual drama of kingship

To complete our survey of pharaonic sources on the myth of kingship we ought to mention two documents that appear to be ritual dramas enacted during state or temple ceremonies. They differ from the Edfu drama in being universal in conception and less concerned with graphic descriptions of the

Relief from the drama depicting the triumph of the god Horus over the god Seth in the form of a hippopotamus. Outer ambulatory of the Temple of Edfu, Ptolemaic period.

humbling of Seth. The first is inscribed on the Shabaka Stone, our source of information about the Memphite creation legend.

On the stone a section deals with the judgement of Horus and Seth in a form involving dialogue between the gods and a scribe's explanatory notes. The earth god Geb is the presiding judge at the tribunal of gods. His first decision attempts to reconcile the claims of the two plaintiffs: Seth will rule over Upper Egypt, to include his birthplace of Su, while Horus will have Lower Egypt, to include a site where, according to another tradition, Osiris drowned in the Nile. 'Geb said to Horus and Seth "I have separated you".' But Geb then decides that Horus (editorial gloss here: 'he is the son of his son, his firstborn') should have a greater portion than Seth. Consequently he awards Horus the inheritance of all Egypt. Horus then is acclaimed as the 'Uniter of his land' at Memphis and equated with the Memphite deity 'Ta-tenen, south of the wall, lord of eternity'. Finally, the concept of Horus, now wearing the crowns of Upper and Lower Egypt, as uniter of the two lands is emphasised.

We now pass onto the Ramesseum Dramatic Papyrus, now in the British Museum, discovered at Thebes in 1895 and dating to the Middle Kingdom. It is an elaborate document consisting of 138 columns of text complemented by a series of over thirty vignettes along the lower edge. The event that had occasioned its compilation was the Jubilee Festival of King Senwosret I (1971–1926 BC), although the surviving papyrus dates from the time of Amenemhat III four reigns later (1844–1797 BC). The forty-six separate scenes of this drama follow a definite pattern: first, a statement of the action; second, the mythological explanation of its meaning; then the conversation between the gods with the pharaoh himself acting the role of Horus; and finally, stage directions. If we isolate the elements relating to the transmission of kingship we begin with the possession of the Sacred Eye (the most powerful amuletic symbol in ancient Egypt) by Horus – the episode of his loss of sight after Seth's attack is glossed over. Then a scene concerns the punishment of cattle for trampling on Osiris in his role as god of grain: oxen are treading barley in order to thresh it and Horus orders them to desist – 'Do not beat this, my father'. The oxen have to continue so that bread can be made but they are beaten as supporters of Seth. The drama also includes mock combat between Horus and Seth with Geb urging the cessation of hostilities.

In reviewing the king's regalia we come across a few significant points not brought out in the myth so far. The monarch has two sceptres which become interpreted as an absorption into the royal person of the strength of his enemy Seth. This refers to the legend of Seth being wounded in his testicles, a counterbalance to the injury to Horus' eyes: Thoth exhorts Horus to assume his enemy's power by taking up the two sceptres which represent Seth's testicles. Also in the drama the king wears a ritual corselet called the *Qeni*. This embodies all the immortal vitality of Osiris, and by strapping the *Qeni* to his chest and back the monarch symbolically enacts a union between the murdered Osiris and his avenging son Horus.

Plutarch's version

The Greek writer Plutarch (AD *c.* 40–*c.* 120) compiled a volume called *Peri Isidos Kai Osiridos*, Concerning Isis and Osiris, probably a few years before his death. He dedicated it to Klea, a priestess at Delphi who seems likely to have been a devotee of Isis. Plutarch's work is a rich amalgam of Egyptian traditions surviving in earlier writers like Manetho, a priestly historian who lived during the reigns of the first two Ptolemies, or Hekataios of Abdera (*fl.* 300 BC), combined with Greek speculations as found in Pythagoras (*fl. c.* 530 BC), Plato (429–347 BC), the Stoics (*fl. c.* 300 BC) and Gnostics (*fl. c.* AD 200). Plutarch covers topics such as the purification rituals of the priests, the cult of the synthetic Graeco-Egyptian deity Sarapis and animal cults. The following account of the myth of kingship, using the Greek names of the gods, is preserved by Plutarch.

The god Kronos (Geb) and the goddess Rhea (Nut) had illicit intercourse. Helios (the sun god) tried to prevent Rhea from giving birth at any time in the year. However, Hermes (Thoth) managed to add five days to the year by beating the moon in a game of draughts. These became the birthdays of five deities – Osiris, Apollo (Horus the Elder), Typhon (Seth), Isis and Nephthys. Later, the kingship of Osiris dragged the Egyptians out of savagery and into civilisation: he taught people how to cultivate the fields and establish laws; he journeyed through the world, turning people towards civilised communities not by force of arms but through eloquence and song. On his return Typhon devised a plot with seventy-two fellow-conspirators to overthrow Osiris. They had an exquisitely decorated chest made, exactly to the measurements of Osiris. At a banquet Typhon offered the chest to whomever fitted inside it and suspicion was allayed by lots of people trying it. Of course when Osiris got inside the lid was slammed down and bolted. The chest was thrown into the Tanitic branch of the Nile and carried out into the Mediterranean sea. Isis wandered around in a state of distress and eventually learned of the fate of the chest. During her peregrinations, incidentally, she adopted the jackal god Anubis as her guardian – apparently unperturbed that he was the offspring of an illicit liaison between her sister Nephthys and Osiris. She pursued the chest to Byblos in the Lebanon where it had been enveloped in a magnificent heath-tree which the king had cut down to form a pillar in his palace. Isis sat by a fountain and befriended the handmaids of the queen of Byblos. She breathed on their skin a fragrance which drew the attention of the queen who sent for Isis and made her the nurse of her young son. At night, in order to give the child immortality, Isis set fire to him and in the shape of a swallow flew around the pillar in which the chest containing Osiris was hidden. Her laments brought the queen to the room, and she had hysterics when she saw her son on fire. This understandable reaction broke the magic of the spell. Isis then demanded the pillar and cut out the chest, donating the outer wood, which was coated with fragrant unguent and wrapped in linen, to her temple at Byblos. She brought the chest back to Egypt but neglected it on one occasion when she went to visit her son Apollo (already born in this version) who was being brought up in Buto. By chance that night Typhon was out hunting and came across the chest. He cut the body of Osiris into fourteen pieces and scattered them throughout the land. Isis went in a papyrus skiff in search of each part and held a burial ceremony wherever she found one. This accounts for the numerous tombs of Osiris claimed at different sanctuaries in Egypt. Isis failed to recover his phallus which Typhon had thrown in the Nile and which had provided a meal for the lepidotus, phragus and oxyrhynchus fish.

Osiris himself had trained Apollo for battle, and when he came up from the underworld, he was satisfied that Apollo was determined to avenge him. The battle between Typhon and Apollo lasted for many days, but Apollo proved the victor at last. Apollo was angered at Isis who led Typhon in bonds but then freed him. He ripped the crown off Isis' head but Hermes replaced it with the cow-horn head-dress – an insignia shared by Isis and Hathor. Typhon tried to get a charge of illegitimacy against Apollo but the gods did not approve, and Typhon was vanquished in two more battles. And thus ends Plutarch's account of the myth of kingship.

Isis 'Great in Magic'

The goddess Isis had a well-earned reputation for exceptional guile, tenacity and cleverness. Several myths reflecting these characteristics survive in magical cults written on papyrus scrolls or in a most elaborate form carved on stelae. The stories of Isis comprise the spells of healing so pertinent to the daily life of ordinary Egyptians, the common ailments, fears and threats which preoccupied them: such as childbirth, fevers, headaches, gastric disorders; crocodiles, snakes, scorpions and malicious worms.

Some spells clearly form an integral element in physicians' manuals and were meant to be recited over a patient. One device aimed at alleviating pain was to identify the sick person with a figure in mythology eventually cured by the intervention of a powerful deity. For example, in a spell designed to relieve the pain of stomach cramps the sick person is called Horus in his form of a young child. The mother represents Isis and concludes that the agony stems from alien worms which have to be driven out. Consequently nineteen magical signs are drawn on the tender regions of the abdomen in order to force the parasites out of the body. Similarly, in a British Museum Medical papyrus (no. 10059), the ingenuity of Isis cures a fever or a burn in the following way. The patient becomes the young Horus scorched in the desert. Isis arrives and asks if water is available; she is given a negative reply. 'Never mind', she asserts, 'water is within my mouth and a Nile flood between my thighs'. This spell is recited over a concoction of human milk, gum and cat hairs, which is then applied to the sufferer. Thus the patient's fever or burns are cooled.

Isis and the seven scorpions

From an elaborate compilation of spells and amuletic vignettes carved on the Metternich Stela (Metropolitan Museum, New York) we can unravel the myth of Isis and the seven scorpions. The purpose of including this story on the stela was to protect the owner against the ever-present danger of a scorpion bite. The scene at the beginning finds Isis weaving the mummy shroud for her husband Osiris, murdered by Seth who wanted his throne. Thoth, god of wisdom, advises Isis to go into hiding with her young son Horus. She must protect Horus against Seth's machinations and raise him to adulthood to avenge Osiris' murder.

The myth of kingship on the stela now gives way to the relating of

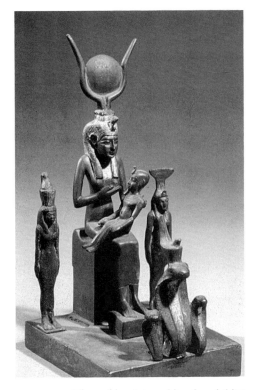

ABOVE LEFT *The goddess Isis suckling her child Horus, a symbol of her protective magical powers. Late-Period bronze.*

ABOVE RIGHT *Upper part of the Metternich stela depicting Horus as a child. It is inscribed with magical texts that were recited to cure ailments and to protect against animal bites. One such text recounts Horus' cure of poisonous bites by the god Thoth.*

Isis' magical powers to cure venomous stings. Isis leaves her house in the evening with an escort of seven scorpions. (Incidentally, seven is a number of tremendous potency in Egyptian magic – for example, seven knots are required in procedures to cure headaches or postnatal breast problems.) Three of the scorpions, Petet, Tjetet and Matet, precede Isis and ensure that her path is safe. Under her palanquin are two more scorpions, Mesetet and Mesetetef, while the remaining two, Tefen and Befen, protect the rear. Isis impresses upon the scorpions the need for extreme caution so that they do not alert Seth to their whereabouts. She even instructs them not to get into conversation with anyone they meet on the way. It is hard at this point to suppress amusement at the bizarre image of a loquacious scorpion exchanging pleasantries with a perplexed Egyptian villager. Eventually Isis reaches her destination of the Town of the Two Sisters in the Nile Delta. A wealthy noblewoman sees the strange party arrive and quickly shuts the door of her house. The seven scorpions all find this extremely galling and plot their revenge on the inhospitable woman. In preparation, six scorpions load their individual poisons on the sting of the seventh, Tefen.

The temple of Isis on the island of Philae as seen by the 19th-century artist David Roberts. Now transported to the neighbouring island of Agilkia, this temple was the last to hold out against the advent of Christianity. Ptolemaic and Roman period.

Meanwhile, a humble peasant girl offers Isis the haven of her simple house. This girl is of course the counterpart to the unfriendly wealthy woman, allowing for an unobtrusive touch of social comment in the structure of the story. Next we find that Tefen has crawled under the door of the wealthy woman's house and has stung her son. Distraught, the woman roams around the town seeking help for her child who is on the verge of death. Her inhospitability to Isis is now repaid because no-one answers her calls for assistance. However, Isis, in Egyptian eyes the supreme example of a devoted mother, cannot tolerate the death of an innocent child and undertakes to revive the woman's son. Holding the boy she utters words of great magical power. Naming each of the scorpions, thereby dominating them, Isis causes their combined poison to become ineffectual in the child. By extension the words of her spell will be applicable to any child suffering a scorpion sting, if recited together with the administering of a 'medical prescription' of barley-bread, garlic and salt. Once over her distress and seeing her son healthy, the woman who had refused Isis shelter becomes contrite: she brings out her worldly wealth and makes a present of it to Isis and to the peasant girl who had shown true Egyptian hospitality to a stranger.

Isis and the secret nature of the sun god

The underlying feature of this myth is to emphasise both the potency of Isis' magic and the power that derives from the knowledge of the quintessential personality of a name. It is preserved through its use as a spell to 'ward off poison'. Its source is Papyrus 1993 in the Turin Museum and it dates to Dynasty XIX (*c.* 1200 BC), although a more fragmentary version survives in Papyrus Chester Beatty XI in the British Museum (no. 10691).

The character of Isis is succinctly portrayed at the start of the myth: 'Isis was a clever woman ... more intelligent than countless gods ... she was ignorant of nothing in heaven or on earth'. Her scheme was to discover the secret name of the sun god, the supreme deity, and it would, if successful, rank her and her son Horus next to him at the head of the pantheon.

Her plan was to wound the sun god with his own strength. Every day he journeyed across the firmament from the Eastern to the Western Horizon in his 'Boat of Millions' (i.e. Millions of Years). In this myth the sun god, progressing in years, is unflatteringly depicted as letting his mouth drop open on one occasion (possibly through nodding-off to sleep) and dribbling saliva to the ground. This was the chance that Isis was waiting for. She mixed his saliva with earth and used her magic to fashion out of it a live venomous snake. Knowing the habits of the sun god, Isis left the snake at the crossroads by which he would pass when he came out for a stroll from his palace which he used when visiting Egypt. As planned, the snake bit the sun god who immediately felt a furnace raging inside him. He yelled out to the sky and his Ennead came rushing to discover the problem. The sun god, bitten by his own venom, was trembling all over as the poison took hold of him: 'You gods who originated from me ... something painful has attacked me but I do not know its nature. I did not see it with my eyes. I did not create it with my hand ... There is no agony to match this'. The other gods, despite the hopes of the supreme deity that their magic and wisdom might cure him, can only mourn his lost vigour, the source of all life. The dramatic entrance of Isis oozing sympathy gives the sun god hope and he relates his misfortune to her. He is in a bad way – freezing and burning at the same time, sweating, shivering and sporadically losing his vision.

Isis now proposes her deal – her magic in exchange for his secret name. For him to divulge his exclusive name would mean a loss of prestige and the insecurity of someone else knowing his hidden nature and quintessential identity. So he prevaricates and reels off many of his other names:

> Creator of the heavens and the earth
> Moulder of the Mountains
> Creator of the water for the 'Great Flood' [primeval cow goddess]
> Maker of the bull for the cow in order to bring sexual pleasure into being
> Controller of the Inundation
> Khepri in the morning
> Re at noon
> Atum in the evening.

Isis indicates that his secret name was not included and seems to intensify the raging poison. Finally, the sun god can take the torment no longer and acquiesces. He agrees to tell her his secret name on the understanding that she in turn binds her son Horus with an oath not to divulge it to any other being. It is worth noting that since the pharaoh of Egypt was the manifestation of the god Horus then he too would share in this powerful knowledge. Infuriatingly, the papyrus scroll does not reveal the name that the sun god told Isis but proceeds to give the words of the spell the goddess recited to cure him – a formula which, if accompanied by a draught of 'scorpion's herb' mixed with beer or wine, will heal anyone suffering from a poisonous sting.

The myth of cataclysm

The myth of cataclysm is a major example of the temporary disturbance of the rapport between gods and mankind. The underlying factors were the deep suspicions of the sun god towards men and the over-reaching confidence of the human race – the result was rebellion and a cata-strophic death toll.

The relationship between the human race and the gods depended on a myriad of diverse microcosms scattered throughout the Nile Valley. These were the temples, each governed by a hierarchy of priests. The priests' responsi-bilities, entrusted to them by the pharaoh, included daily rituals of reciting religious formulae and providing victuals in the sanctuary. If this service was performed correctly and no offerings were deficient then the gods and god-desses in each temple would feel satisfied and act benignly towards Egypt.

The detailed liturgy which a High Priest delivered was a response to the order of the universe established by the creator god at the beginning of time. This cosmic structure was personified as Maat, the goddess of truth, right and orderly conduct. Pharaohs are frequently shown holding her effigy, the form of a kneeling woman with an ostrich-feather on her head, to indicate their allegiance to the laws of the creator god. All the stages of making an offering or attending to the divine statue were rigorously documented on temple papyri. On the walls of the temples themselves it is the pharaoh who can be seen symbolically carrying out the requisite rituals in the inner sanctum, in a way visually indicating personal responsibility for the actions of his appointed representatives in the higher echelons of the priesthood.

This system created a mood of optimism in the people, who believed that the deities of the Egyptian pantheon were on the side of the human race. Individuals could of course transgress and be punished by a god or goddess as a result of their misdemeanour. Fine examples of this lapse of respect towards the gods, dating to Dynasty XIX (c. 1307–1196 BC), are found in the stelae from the village of workers on the royal tombs, known today as Deir el-Medina. Originally dedicated in local temples, these stelae reflect penitence for human errors and humbly request the offended deity for release from punishment. The draughtsman Neferabu managed to upset a god and a goddess on separate occasions and left votive stelae to them emphasising his contrition. On one stela, in the Turin Museum, Neferabu has clearly offended Meretseger, 'she who loves silence', a snake goddess residing on the peak overlooking the royal necropolis for which she was responsible.

For his offence, not specified, Meretseger caused Neferabu to be in agony – his pain is likened to the last stages of pregnancy. Eventually the goddess relented and brought 'sweet breezes' to cure him. On the other stela, in the British Museum, Neferabu admits that he took an oath in the name of the god Ptah Lord of Maat but swore falsely. Consequently, the god caused Neferabu to see 'darkness by day' – he struck him blind. Neferabu professes the justice of Ptah's action and begs for mercy from the god.

It was also possible for a monarch to govern in a way that upset the gods. The reign of the pharaoh Akhenaten (1353–1335 BC) saw the supremacy of the sun disc, called the Aten, the closure of temples and the eclipse of the traditional pantheon, including Amun-Re. When his son Tutankhamun succeeded to the throne of Egypt there was a reversal of Akhenaten's policies and the established temples were back in business. On a stela set up in the Karnak temple (now in the Cairo Museum) the pharaoh describes the mood of the traditional gods at the excesses of Akhenaten:

... the temples of the gods and goddesses ... were in ruins. Their shrines were deserted and overgrown. Their sanctuaries were as non-existent and their courts were used as roads ... the gods turned their backs upon this land ... If anyone made a prayer to a god for advice he would never respond – and the same applied to a goddess. Their hearts ached inside them and they inflicted damage left right and centre.

The restorations made by Tutankhamun, particularly for Amun-Re and Ptah, rectified the distress throughout the land and the gods and goddesses once again became favourable towards Egypt.

The cataclysm myth survives as an element in a corpus of magical spells called the *Book of the Divine Cow* aimed at protecting the body of the sovereign. The earliest copy of sections of this book is found on the interior of the outermost of the four gilded shrines that fitted over the sarcophagus of Tutankhamun (r. 1333–1323 BC), originally in his tomb in the Valley of the Kings and now in the Cairo Museum. There is a longer version of this text in a side room off the sarcophagus-chamber of the tomb of Sety I in the royal valley. Other royal tombs from the Nineteenth and Twentieth Dynasties carry portions of this work so that we can put together a reasonably full account of the myth. The role of the Divine Cow will become clear as the sequel to the myth of cataclysm.

The scene is set in the era when Egypt was under the direct rule of the sun god Re. This period is of course unquantifiable in terms of history and belongs to a remote mythological past – although it is interesting to note that an important historical papyrus (the Turin Royal Canon) and Manetho's survey of dynasties begin with Egypt under the kingship of a series of gods, before the unification of the country under the first pharaoh around 3000 BC. In an infuriatingly unspecific manner, the *Book of the Divine Cow* describes the human race as 'plotting evil plans' against Re – possibly there was the feeling that he had grown too old to govern. Certainly, later in historical times, pharaohs took elaborate precautions to avoid the impression that age was against them being effective rulers: the essence of the Jubilee

The lioness goddess Sakhmet, the instrument of vengeance used by the sun god against mankind. Black granite statue from the precinct of the temple of the goddess Mut at Karnak, c. 1350 BC.

Festivals lay in ceremonies designed to rejuvenate the prowess of the monarch, and the presence of the sun god was conjured up in the imagery of a temple cult-statue whose bones were of silver, flesh of gold and hair of lapis lazuli. Learning of mankind's plot against him Re summons a secret council of the gods in his Great Palace, and is apparently unwilling to warn the human race.

Re first addresses Nu, the primeval material out of which he arose at the time of creation. In his statement he mentions how mankind emerged from the tears of his eyes – a pun on the similar sound between 'men' and 'tear' in the Egyptian language (i.e. a phoneme) – and now they are conspiring against him. He wants to know Nu's opinion before he kills the entire human race. Nu's reply is that the Eye of Re, the solar eye, will be the instrument to terrorise and slay mankind. Re now becomes aware that men know he is angry over their plot and discovers that they have fled into the deserts of Egypt. The gods in unison urge Re to take vengeance on the conspirators.

The symbol of the Eye of Re is complex but an underlying feature of it is that it can form an entity independent of the sun god himself – even to the extent of going off on journeys to remote regions and having to be enticed back. Here the Eye of Re becomes his daughter, the goddess Hathor. Most often we find Hathor in the role of a divine mother-figure to the pharaoh, suckling him with her milk, as a guardian of the Theban necropolis or as the goddess of love and joy whom the Greeks equated with Aphrodite. In the myth of cataclysm, however, Hathor becomes a deity of invincible destructive powers, pursuing men in the desert and slaughtering them. When she returns to Re she exults in the lust for blood, glorying in the massacre. To complicate the nature of the Eye of Re the myth now explains how Hathor became transformed into the goddess Sakhmet – a ferocious leonine deity whose name means the 'Powerful One'. Thus the myth provides us with the vivid imagery of a raging lioness wading in blood who savaged mankind in an ecstasy of slaughter.

The Eye of Re now rests, recuperating her strength for further killing the next day. But the sun god himself has changed his mood from vengeance to sympathy for mankind. We are given no clues as to the reason for this transformation. Possibly it is the realisation that the temples of Egypt would be without their priestly occupants and consequently their altars would be empty of offerings for the gods. The cosmic pattern that the creator god had established would thus become deficient. Possibly the *volte-face* had to do with the reluctance of Re to consign beings created out of matter from himself (i.e. his tears) to oblivion. This last possibility would be in keeping with the Egyptian belief that no element of the body ought to be alientated into another's possession or destroyed – hence the four funerary jars to contain the organs eviscerated as part of the process of mummification.

Whatever the reason, Re organises the rescue of mankind from the fierce and merciless goddess whose blood-lust is totally beyond control. The gods only have the night to save the human race before the goddess wakes up. Re therefore sends his personal messengers to run at top speed – the Egyptian says 'to run like the body's shadow' – to Aswan and bring back a large quantity of red ochre. He then tells no less a personage than the 'One of the sidelock of Heliopolis', an epithet for the High Priest of the sun god, to squeeze the red ochre into a substance that slave girls can mix with barley beer. Soon seven thousand jars of this popular drink have been filled with beer that looks like human blood. Towards the end of the night Re and his entourage carry the jars to the place where the goddess will come to continue her slaughter and there they flood the region with the blood-beer to a height of 'three palms', about 22.5 cm. In the morning the goddess sees the 'blood' and, rejoicing in the unexpected bonus, drinks deeply and becomes intoxicated. As a result she fails to find the remainder of mankind left over from the previous massacre.

The rest of this compilation, following the punishment and near extermination of the human race, is concerned primarily with the rebirth and ascension of the sun god, and therefore of the monarch, into heaven on the back of the 'Divine Cow'. Both the shrine of Tutankhamun and the tomb of Sety I have depictions of the Cow 'Mehet wer' or 'Great Flood' who forms the celestial firmament, identifying with the sky goddess Nut. Thus Re, now a cynical sun god and weary of mankind, eventually leaves Egypt. But it is not a total abdication of responsibility because Re appoints Thoth, god of wisdom, as his regent or deputy to keep control of the human race. From Thoth, on the orders of Re, people are given knowledge of the 'sacred words' (i.e. hieroglyphs) in which all scientific wisdom, medicine and mathematics are embodied.

The underworld journey
of the sun god

From 1492 to 1070 BC almost all pharaohs were buried in the royal necropolis on the West Bank of Thebes, fittingly described today as the Valley of the Kings. The rock-cut sepulchres originally contained valuable funerary equipment and the sarcophagi held royal mummies decorated with exquisite jewellery. Despite the venomous sting of Meretseger, the snake goddess dwelling on the peak dominating the valley, and the (erratic) vigilance of the necropolis guards, tomb robbers were able to plunder the treasures of the pharaohs – including a few items from the burial of Tutankhamun which, after being resealed, miraculously escaped being looted until Howard Carter's excavation in 1922. Thankfully there existed no ancient illegal art market demanding fragments of the complicated and confusing designs painted on the walls of the royal tombs. However, these paintings were left to suffer the ravages of the salt inherent in the Theban limestone, occasional torrents of rain and the scrawls in some instances of Greek and Coptic tourists nearly two thousand years ago. It is on these walls that there survives a rich panorama, in spite of the natural damage or multilations, of the Egyptian underworld.

The fertile imagination of the ancient Egyptian religious speculators evolved numerous images and symbols, the sum total of which would emphasise the security of the sun god on his underworld journey and his transformation from the god who descended into the dark regions of the netherworld each night into a regenerated deity emerging each dawn, full of energy and life. Manu was the western mountain where Re began his journey after setting; Duat was the underworld through which he travelled; Bakhu was the eastern mountain above which he rose in the morning.

Three major compositions survive which depict the dangers successfully negotiated by Re in the underworld and dispel doubts about his safe emergence into the sky. These complex compilations evolved over centuries and acquired additions which often obscure rather than elucidate enigmatic scenes or texts. Sometimes the ancient scribal draughtsmen were unable to make sense of their working documents which accumulated over generations, with the consequence that some inscriptions read as exotic gibberish. On other occasions sheets of the papyri scrolls may have suffered extensive wear and tear and become too illegible to copy onto the wall. In these cases the draughtsmen

LEFT *Underworld scene showing the sky goddess Nut and birth symbolism. Tomb of Ramesses* VI, *Valley of the Kings, c. 1150* BC.

BELOW *'Flesh of Re'. Ram-headed form of the sun god, protected by a gigantic snake, journeying in his boat through the underworld. Valley of the Kings, c. 1300* BC.

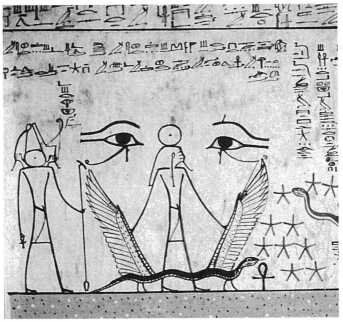

'Sacred Eyes' and a winged snake with legs beside a two-headed figure wearing the red and white crowns of united Egypt. An image from the Book of Am-Duat in the tomb of Tuthmosis III *(1479–1425* BC*), Valley of the Kings.*

wrote into the composition the hieroglyphs *Gem Wesh* meaning 'original source found defective'. The earliest of these compilations is the *Book of Am-Duat*, the 'Book of What is in the Underworld'. Visitors to the tombs of Tuthmosis III (1425 BC) and Amenhotep II (1401 BC) can see complete versions of this book in the schematic designs on the walls of the burial chambers. The tombs of Sety I (1290 BC) and Ramesses VI (1143 BC) have eleven out of twelve scenarios, these scenarios symbolising the twelve hours of the night. The second composition, the *Book of Gates*, can be found in part in its earliest appearance in the tomb of Horemheb (1307 BC) but the fullest versions are in the tomb of Ramesses VI and on the immaculately carved sarcophagus of Sety I which, having been turned down by the then niggardly Trustees of the British Museum, was purchased by Sir John Soane and can be inspected in his museum in Lincoln's Inn Fields in London. In the tomb of Ramesses VI there is a complete copy of the latest and rarest of these three compositions known as the *Book of Caverns*.

The Book of Am-Duat

The sun god makes his underworld journey through Twelve Scenarios, to become reborn as Khepri the scarab-beetle. At the outset of his journey the sun god is at the Western Horizon approaching the River of Wernes along which he will travel. In a prologue the essence of this composition emphasising its magical power is formulated: 'Knowledge of the power of those in the underworld. Knowledge of their actions – knowing the sacred rituals for Re, knowing the hidden dynamism, knowing the hours and gods, knowing the gates and paths where the great god passes, knowing the powerful and the destroyed'.

Re starts his journey through the First Scenario (or Hour) of Duat and is depicted as a ram-headed god in a shrine and is called 'Flesh'. This description highlights the netherworld form of Re which will eventually transmute into Khepri. He travels in his solar boat and his crew consists of two gods at the prow named 'Path-opener' and 'Mind', as well as a goddess called the 'Lady of the Boat' who wears cow horns and a sun-disc, hawk-headed 'Horus the Adorer' and, by the steering oars, four deities named 'Bull of Truth', 'Vigilant', 'Will' and 'Guide of the Boat'. On either side of Re are groups of deities shown in individual squares – for example, there are two sets of nine baboons who open the doors for Re and sing to him as he enters the underworld, and twelve serpent goddesses who light up the darkness.

Re sails into the Second Hour of Night where he establishes landrights for the grain gods of the region of Wernes. The Third Hour is when Re revives Osiris by giving him 'Will' and 'Mind' – energy to decide and act. In the Fourth Scenario a distinctive motif appears in the form of a slanted passageway with two open doors. There are guardian snakes, some from the realm of mythical beings possessing a human head and four short legs, or three snake heads and two wings. That these snakes will not harm Re or his entourage is confirmed by magical epithets indicating their self-suf-ficiency in food: 'living on the breath of his mouth' or 'living on the voice of the gods guarding the road'. The passage is the way to the underworld from the traditional entrance of 'Ro-setau, or 'Gate of the passageways'. Through this route is access to the body of Sokar, a necropolis-god of Memphis, and to the tomb of Osiris.

In the Fifth Hour Re has reached a crucial stage on his journey and one which is full of imagery of resurrection. The solar boat is towed towards a mound out of which a head emerges called 'Flesh of Isis who is above the sand of the land of Sokar'. Below is the interior of this mound across which Re is being towed. Its gate is guarded by four heads spurting flames. A pellet of sand rests on the back of the two-headed leonine earth god Aker. Emerging out of this is Sokar, hawk-headed, standing on the back of a serpent with a human head at one end and three snake heads at the other. Sokar here is the manifestation of the underworld body of Re in a primeval form, animated by the passing of the sun god above. The tow-rope is actually held over the mound of Sokar by a scarab beetle emerging from a desert mound in the upper register of the painting. Isis and Nephthys in the shape of kites flank this mound which represents the desert tomb of Osiris. Again the sun god is overcoming death by emerging from the mound called 'Night' as Khepri the scarab-beetle – a visual representation of the belief of the Egyptian theologians that life and death are a continual cycle without one suppressing the other. In this image of the mound the sun god is contained in Osiris but not restricted in 'permanent' death.

During the Sixth Hour Re in his boat comes to a halt before a seated representation of the god Thoth as a baboon holding a sacred ibis. Thoth's purpose is to found a city for the gods in the fields and for the kings of Upper and Lower Egypt. Here also is depicted the body of Khepri encoiled within a five-headed serpent – the sun god visits his manifestation as an underworld corpse. This possibly appears bizarre to our rationality so here are a few sentences from a synthesis made by a Dutch scholar called Kristensen which might clarify the thought processes of the Egyptians on life and death:

... all that lives and all that grows is the result of an inexplicable and completely mysterious cooperation of heterogeneous factors ... Life and Death appear to be irreconcilable opposites: yet together they form everlasting life. Neither predominates; they alternate or, most aptly, they produce one another. Universal life is the totality of death and life; in it hostile forces are reconciled and have abandoned their individual independence ... the sun, when it goes down, does not die but reaches the hidden fountain of its life. Becoming or arriving is the nature of Khepri ... But every arising occurs in and from death, which thus appears to be potential life. Darkness is the cradle of light; in it the sun finds the power to arise ... Absolute life has its home in the realm of death.
(Quoted by N. Rambova in A. Piankoff, 'Mythological Papyrus: texts', in *Bollingen Series* XL.3 [Pantheon Books 1957] pp. 29–30)

Some violent scenes follow in the Seventh Hour as Re sails through. Protected by the coils of a snake is a god called 'Flesh of Osiris', in front of whom

The cat of the sun god symbolically decapitates Apophis, the underworld snake of chaos. Tomb of Nakht-Amun (c. 1290 BC), Deir el-Medina, Western Thebes.

a knife-brandishing deity with feline ears has decapitated enemies, while another – the 'Punisher' – holds rebels caught in a rope. The opponents of Osiris have been captured and annihilated. Before Re in the solar boat is the scene of his arch-enemy Apophis being overthrown. Apophis is a gigantic snake symbolising the force of non-existence and a perpetual threat to the sun god whom he attempts to swallow. Despite the indestructibility of Apophis, the representations on the royal tomb walls attempt to vanquish him by magic so that he appears in a state of being destroyed or subdued whenever the sun god is in his vicinity. There the snake lies extended for about 240 m. The scorpion-goddess Serket and the god called 'Director of the Knives' hold the head and tail of Apophis whose head and body are pierced with knife blades.

In the Eighth Hour Re is towed, with nine symbols of his power before him in the form of human-headed staves to which is attached a package from which emerges a knife. These emblems destroy his enemies. Around are gated compartments where various deities are shown accompanied by the sign for linen clothing. Some of these figures are mummiform; some are seated with human heads; others with the head of a bull, goat, rat, ichneumon, crocodile or hippopotamus; and others take the form of cobras. They respond to the call of Re as he passes by their 'caverns' with a variety of cries likened, for example, to tom-cats, a river bank falling into the Nile flood, or a nest of birds. In the Ninth Hour Re meets twelve fire-spitting cobras who guard Osiris and who 'live on the blood of those whom they slaughter'. He also sails past gods holding palm-branch sceptres who are responsible for carving trees or plants.

In the Tenth Hour symbols appear of the imminent resurrection of Re at dawn. The scarab beetle holds the egg from which he will emerge in the

Eastern Horizon and two sun disks are shown ready to be propelled into the sky. In front of the solar boat an armed escort of twelve gods checks the security of the approach to the Eastern Horizon. Re addresses them: 'Be swift with your arrows, target your spears and draw your bows. Punish my enemies lurking in the darkness near the gate'. The Eleventh Hour graphically depicts the destruction of these underworld enemies who are thrown into the fire pits, each with a goddess spitting fire into it. These enemies are shown as bound captives, as destroyed souls, as shadows and as lopped-off heads. In a sixth, larger pit four rebels are shown upside-down. Horus makes a speech over this wholesale massacre: '... you are fallen into fiery pits and cannot escape ... the knife of she who directs the knife blades slashes into you, she cuts you to bits and butchers you. You will never see the ones who live on earth'.

Now the sun god has reached the Twelfth Hour and the climax of his journey through the underworld. The solar boat is towed into the tail of a gigantic serpent in whose body Re sheds his underworld manifestation and is born out of the snake's mouth as Khepri the scarab beetle. In this shape Re rests above the head of the air god Shu whose arms seal the underworld. Re then sails up from the East in the day boat to 'shine between the thighs of Nut'.

Tabulation of the sun god's progress in the Am-Duat

Scenario	Name of underworld city/region	Name of the Hour goddess
1	Great City	Splitter of the heads of Re's enemies
2	Field of Wernes	The Wise, Guardian of her lord
3	Field of the Grain gods and Water of Osiris	Slicer of Souls
4	Cavern of the Life of Forms	Great of Power
5	Cavern of Sokar	She on her boat
6	Deep Water	Proficient leader
7	Cavern of Osiris, City of the Mysterious Cave	Repeller of the Snake
8	City of the God's Sarcophagi	Mistress of the Night
9	City of the Living Manifestations	Adorer
10	City of Deep Water and Steep Banks	Beheader of Rebels
11	City of Corpse-Counting	The Star, repulser of rebels
12	Cavern at the end of darkness, City of the Appearance of Birth	Beholder of the beauty of Re

The Book of Caverns

This latest compilation glorifies the sun god as bringer of life and brightness into the dark realm of the underworld, envisaged as a sequence of caverns. The paintings depict Re progressing through Duat, illuminating the caverns of the gods; they also show the penalty for enemies and rebels in gruesome detail. This interplay of good fortune against just punishments makes the *Books of Caverns* a psychological tableau. It stands apart from the other underworld compositions in its intensity of concentration on reward and punishment. Overall, the effect is one of remembering the vivid execution of the enemies when perhaps the benefits of the journey of Re should be paramount.

The beginning shows Re on foot descending into the underworld. He is confronted with a series of ovals containing figures of gods and goddesses. Each oval is a sarcophagus enveloping a body which the power of Re can

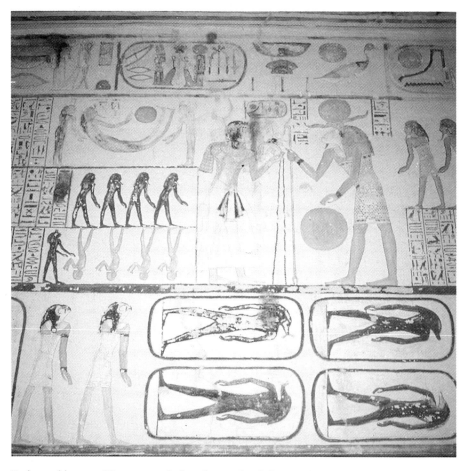

Underworld scene of Ramesses VI before the ram-headed sun god, amid gods in shrines and defeated enemies hanging upside down. Valley of the Kings, c. 1150 BC.

vivify on his journey. In the First Cavern Re demonstrates his knowledge of secret names to ward off danger and attack by identifying the guardian deities. For example, here are some of the terms he uses to address three huge serpents:

'Stinger in your cavern, frightener – submit and give way! I enter the West to provide for Osiris and place his opponents in the executioner's.

Fearful Visage in your cavern to whom those in the underworld hand over the souls of the place of destruction . . .

Encircler of Rosetau for the ruler of Duat . . .'

The naming of the snake and assertion of his own power enables Re to progress through the cavern, greeting the deities in their sarcophagi. Immediately we follow his path our eyes fall to the lower register of the painting where bound prisoners and decapitated enemies march along.

The punishment continues in the Second Cavern where some upside-down enemies have had their hearts torn out and placed at their feet. Here the sun god meets some gods in their coffins whose heads are those of shrew mice and catfish. These are primeval symbols associated with Horus of Leto-polis and Osiris. Progressing into the Third Cavern Re treads a path across Aker, the two-headed leonine earth god. Below is Osiris depicted as ithyphallic to indicate his revival through the light of Re. A eulogy on his beauty and benefactions greets the sun god in the Fourth Cavern.

In the Fifth Cavern Re witnesses the total annihilation of his opponents. A number of cauldrons are filled with upside-down beheaded corpses, heads, hearts, souls and shadows. Re addresses two goddesses beside one of the cauldrons to ensure that potential as well as past enemies will be similarly executed: 'Goddesses of the powerful flame stirring cauldrons with bones burning the souls, corpses, flesh and shadow of my opponents – Look I pass close to you, I destroy my enemies. You will stay in your caves, your fire will heat my cauldrons, your souls will not abandon here nor join my entour-age'. The Fifth Cavern is, however, visually dominated by two large, standing figures stretching across the height of three registers of paintings. So the sun god will meet 'The Secret One', a representation of Nut, the sky goddess, surrounded by solar disks and images of resurrection. He will also encounter the ithyphallic Osiris.

But now Re has arrived at the Sixth Cavern where his foes are being decapitated. It is time for him to leave the slaughtering behind and the image of the scarab beetle pushing the sun disk prevails in the upper registers of the final scene. Towed towards the Eastern Horizon the boat holds Re repre-sented as the scarab beetle and ram-headed god. The transformation occurs so that the scarab beetle form of the sun god then moves towards the east – but its head has amalgamated with the underworld image of Re so that we see a hybrid solar creature consisting of the body of a scarab beetle and the head of a ram. It is a time of rebirth and therefore the symbol of the sun as a child sucking its finger can be seen resting its foot on the solar disk about to emerge from the Eastern Mountain.

The Book of Gates

This composition is one of the most dramatically presented in royal tombs, notably for its recurring motif of a gigantic serpent spitting fire as it guards a gateway through Duat. A prologue locates the start of the sun god's journey in the Western Desert mountains from where Re passes through a gate protected by a snake into the underworld. Re is represented as anthropomorphic up to his shoulders, which are surmounted by a ram's head and sun disk. He holds the sceptre of dominion. His title is given as the 'Flesh of Re' which is his underworld corporeal manifestation. He stands in his solar boat in a shrine which is surrounded by a serpent with a vast number of coils called 'Mehen' or the 'Encircler'. Also in the boat are two personified qualities of the sun god depicted as standing human male figures — at the prow is Sia or 'Mind'/'Perception' while by the steering oars stands Heka or 'Magic'. The papyriform boat is towed by four dwellers of the underworld. This is the theme of continuity that runs through the whole *Book of Gates* inasmuch as it shows in the central register the sun god's safe journey along the River of Duat. The registers above and below give us glimpses of action on the two banks of the river. In this First Scenario 'Flesh of Re' is towed past his form of Atum, creator god of Heliopolis, who is supervising the destruction of enemies lying prone on the ground or marching in a line of bound captives. Their sins are specified as blasphemy against Re, perjury and murder. Atum speaks to these criminals:

'... I am the son born of his father, I am the father born from his son [i.e. Atum and Re are together in a continual cycle of renewal]. You are bound with strong ropes ... Your bodies will be hacked up, your soul will become non-existent. You will not see Re in his manifestations as he journeys in the secret region'.

The gateways themselves, such as the one Re now passes to enter the Second Scenario, are highly stylised but clearly indicate that they are sturdy double bastions and crenellated with ornaments known as the 'Khekheru' which make their appearance historically in the Step Pyramid complex of King Djoser at Sakkara (*c.* 2600 BC). Nine mummiform gods line the outer walls of the gateway with a special guardian at the entrance and exit of the passageway between the bastions. A fire-spitting cobra rears up above each tower of the gate while a serpent balanced on its tail reaches from the ground to the height of the wall, guarding the actual door. Each of these protective divinities is named so that the sun god merely has to pronounce their identity from his secret knowledge in order to pass safely into the region beyond the gate. In the Second Scenario 'Flesh of Re' greets twelve gods of barley emerging from a lake of fire which acts as a deterrent against birds but by magic does not harm the grain. The boat of the sun god is imagined as passing through a pole with bull-head terminals, representing the Boat of Earth, indicating the power of Re to counter all obstacles by his power to transform himself. On the bank Atum leans on his staff before a hopelessly entangled Apophis, the underworld snake enemy of Re who has here been overthrown.

The sun god is towed past the Third Gate into a region where he sees jackal and cobra gods guarding lakes. The jackal gods protect the Lake of Life from the inhabitants of the underworld because it is sacred and exclusive to the sun god. The Lake of the Cobras guards the flame with which the enemies of Re are annihilated. Also in this region 'Flesh of Re' passes an immensely intricately coiled snake called Hereret. The snake lies in a depression on either side of which are goddesses described as the 'Hours of the Underworld'. Their task is to swallow whatever Hereret might exude or give birth to so that it is rendered harmless.

In the Fourth Scenario a series of twelve gods can be seen on the bank carrying a long rope with extensive lengths of it yet unrolled. Their task is to measure the crops and divide allotted fields among the inhabitants of the underworld. There is general acclaim in the inscriptions that this has been done satisfactorily. On the other bank the god Horus leaning on his staff is preceded by sixteen male figures whom the inscriptions divide into the four traditional races of mankind as perceived through Egyptian eyes: Four Men – these are the 'cattle of Re' in Duat in Egypt and in the deserts, that is, the exclusive element of the human race who can be called Egyptian; Four Middle Easterners – these are the inhabitants of Palestine and Syria whom the lioness goddess Sakhmet is said to have created; Four Nubians – these represent the settled inhabitants and nomadic tribes of regions south of Egypt's natural frontier of the First Cataract of the Nile at Aswan; and Four Libyans – the goddess Sakhmet also created the tribes of the Western Desert and Mediterranean seaboard along the Libyan coast.

The 'Flesh of Re' is now towed past the Fifth Gate and immediately enters the Hall of Osiris. The god Osiris, ruler of Duat, is enthroned on a dais and holds the crook sceptre and ankh, sign of life. Before him on the shoulders of a mummiform deity is a pair of scales for weighing the hearts of those seeking to dwell in Duat in order to judge if their earthly lives have been blameless enough for this privilege. In a papyriform boat a pig is being beaten by an ape, symbolising the humiliation of Seth, the enemy of Osiris. Beyond this hall of the Fifth Scenario the sun god watches the repelling of Apophis who is carried by twelve gods. Human heads emerge from the body of Apophis representing his previous victims and whom Re vivifies. Apophis is described as 'eyeless, noseless, earless, breathing by his roars, living upon his own shouting' in order to symbolise his incapacity for destruction. Further on, twelve gods pull a twisted rope from the mouth of a deity called Aken, each twist representing an hour of the underworld.

'Flesh of Re' is now in the Sixth Scenario, being towed toward poles surmounted by jackal heads to which enemies have been tied ready for beheading. On one bank are gods tending ears of grain and reapers with sickles to provide suitable food and beer offerings for the sun god and Osiris. Beyond the Seventh Gate are gods carrying a rope, from the coils of which emerge emblems like whips, hawk and human heads and stars. These create mysteries in honour of Re but the inscriptions leave us ignorant of the details.

In contrast to the rather staid Seventh Scenario the region beyond the Eighth Gate provides 'Flesh of Re' with the most activity. On the bank he sees the twelve gods who form a council to provide nine souls, shown with bird bodies but human heads and arms, with food on their Island of Flame. He approaches his form of Atum, who leans on his staff contemplating a pool in which men are represented in prone positions. These are water gods connected with the Primeval Flood. Re gives them powers of mobility, breathing and swimming, so that they do not remain static in the element over which they are supposed to exercise benign influence. On the other bank Horus is herding the enemies of Osiris towards a fire-belching snake with mummiform gods emanating from its coils. These enemies have polluted the ceremonies of the god's temple so Horus exhorts the serpent to 'open its jaws, belch out the flame ... burn their corpses, destroy their souls with the conflagration'.

In the Ninth Scenario 'Flesh of Re' follows deities with nets swinging and spearers ready to annihilate Apophis who is lying in wait in the sun god's path. On the bank the sun god sees the crowns of Upper and Lower Egypt and, on the back of a leonine heraldic creature, a god called 'His two faces' consisting of the heads of Horus and Seth placed together on his neck, symbolising the peaceful union of North and South Egypt and hinting at any absence of conflict between the two traditional enemies.

Beyond the Tenth Gate 'Flesh of Re' joins a procession in which another boat travels bearing a front-facing male head. This is the 'Face of the Disk', an element of the sun god himself on its journey to rebirth. On the bank is a dramatic chaining of the snake Apophis. His head is bound by the scorpion goddess Serket who stretches herself full length along the chain. Sixteen gods stand on the snake's back holding the chain and are supported in this task by a massive fist emerging from the ground – no chances are to be taken with this ferocious creature. At the tail end of Apophis stands Osiris, before whom the snaked body rises to show four chained serpent-offspring. Extra protection is provided by five figures on this end coil who represent the earth god Geb and the Sons of Horus.

In the Eleventh Scenario – in addition to the symbolic overthrow and binding of Apophis – four baboons announce the approach of Re in the Eastern Horizon. The final Twelfth Scenario encapsulates the everlasting cycle of the birth of the sun god. From his primeval water the god Nu raises a boat in which travels the sun god as Khepri the scarab beetle and as a disk. Above Nu the sky goddess leans down, her feet resting on the head of Osiris representing Duat. To emphasise the successful completion of his journey a sun disk pushes through the desert sand at the point where Re will rise at dawn.

The three intricate religious compositions just reviewed are often initially puzzling to modern eyes. They can be seen as a medley of garbled inscriptions and an endless roll-call of names. But of course the unhindered journey of the sun god through Duat was a cornerstone of Egyptian belief. Beyond the executions of enemies, the destruction of Apophis, the mummiform deities and the gods in their sarcophagi lies the realm of life. Duat is not a region of despair, and the ancient Egyptian would *not* echo the poem's lines:

> This is the dead land
> This is cactus land
> Here the stone images
> Are raised, here they receive
> The supplication of a dead man's hand
> Under the twinkle of a fading star.
> (from T. S. Eliot, *The Hollow Man*)

These dark sentiments would be rejected because in Duat there is the amalgam of two great gods – Re becomes Osiris and Osiris becomes Re. The underworld god is the past form of the sun god out of whom the sun is born again. In Spell 17 in the *Book of the Dead* we find the following statement and an explanatory gloss:

> 'I am Yesterday, I am Tomorrow
> What does this mean?
> Osiris is Yesterday and Re is Tomorrow'.

The passage of the 'Flesh of Re' through Duat is a process of energising the sun god into Khepri for a new birth. Life and death are a continuum, each eternally engendering the other.

Tabulation of the sun god's journey in the *Book of Gates*

Scenario	Guardian serpent	Name of gate
1	Guardian of the Desert	He of the hidden name (Osiris)
2	Enveloper	Intense of Flame
3	Stinger	Lady of Nourishment
4	Flame-face	One of Action
5	Eye of Flame	Lady of Continuity
6	Darting of Eye	Throne of her Lord
7	Hidden of Eye	Gleaming One
8	Flame-face	Red-hot
9	Earth-tusk	Exalted in Veneration
10	Binder	Sacred
11	Effluent One	Hidden of Access
12	He of the Dawn & Enveloper	Sacred of Power

From history into legend

T he characters in this chapter were each, posthumously, translated from history into legend by becoming the subject of either a cult or a tale. Each can be proved archaeologically to have existed in reality.

Imhotep

Imhotep was the architect of the step pyramid complex of King Djoser (2630–2611 BC) at Sakkara, which in grandeur of concept is unrivalled and which was the first colossal stone edifice to be built. The pyramid suggests a gigantic stairway for the monarch's ascent to the sky, while the surrounding buildings originally provided the temple for the royal cult and pavilions and shrines for the eternal celebration of Djoser's jubilee festivals. A limestone bust from a lost statue of King Djoser (called Netjeri-khet on his monuments) preserves the name and titles of Imhotep:

Seal-bearer of the King of Lower Egypt, one who is near the head of the King [i.e. vizier], Director of the Great Mansion, Royal representative, High Priest of Heliopolis, Imhotep, the carpenter and the sculptor. . . .

From stone vessels discovered in the galleries about 30 m below the pyramid we can add the title 'Chief Lector priest'. Thus, the highest religious and secular offices in the Egyptian administration belonged to Imhotep.

In addition to the pyramid complex Imhotep was the architect of a sanctuary to the sun god at Heliopolis, dedicated by Djoser and surviving today only in fragments of high quality reliefs. His name has also been found in a graffito on the enclosure wall of the unfinished pyramid of King Sekhemkhet (2611–2603 BC), successor to Djoser. This is the latest historical attestation we have for Imhotep so we can assume that he died about 4600 years ago.

His reputation as an experienced architect led to his adoption by the scribes of Egypt as the most eminent practitioner of their craft. He became regarded as a source of intellectual inspiration and a number of moral maxims were alleged to have been committed to papyrus in his name. One reference is in a partly pessimistic, partly hedonistic composition known as the *Harper's song*, the finest copy of which is in Papyrus Harris 500 in the British Museum:

I have heard the words of Imhotep and Hor-dedef [a son of King Khufu] whose maxims are frequently quoted – and what is the state of their monuments now? Their walls are smashed and their places have disappeared – just as if they had never existed.

ABOVE *The step pyramid at Sakkara, constructed by the 'historical' Imhotep for the pharaoh Djoser, c. 2600 BC.*

LEFT *Seated statuette of Imhotep as the embodiment of scribal wisdom. Late-Period bronze.*

If the song was originally written in the reign of a king called Intef, as the introduction boasts, then Imhotep's funerary monument had already become dilapidated or lost by 2000 BC. However, his name lived on in his writings as another document, also in the British Museum, can testify. Its purpose is to extol the professional scribe and it does so by choosing judicious references to illustrate the immortality of literature:

A book is of more value than the house of a master-builder or a tomb in the western desert. ... Is there anyone around today like Hor-dedef? Is there anyone else like Imhotep? ... Those wise men who foretold the future. ... They might be gone and their names fade from memory – except that their writings keep them remembered.

At some point, through a shift in the Egyptian psychological view of the status of Imhotep, his role as a sage became enhanced by attributing his birth to the direct intervention of one of the major gods. Imhotep became 'son of Ptah' creator god of Memphis, whose nature as a god of craftsman particularly suited the fathering of an offspring renowned for sculptural skill. From the Saite period (Dynasty XXVI) there is ample evidence of a vigorous cult centred around Imhotep son of Ptah at Memphis and Sakkara. Hundreds of bronzes depict him in an iconography which subtly emphasise his wisdom and divine parent. He is represented seated with a papyrus scroll across his knees, wearing a skullcap and a long linen kilt. We can interpret the papyrus as suggesting the sources of knowledge kept by scribes in the 'House of Life'. The headgear identifies Imhotep with Ptah, and his priestly linen garment symbolises his religious purity.

His main temple was in North Sakkara with a subsidiary sanctuary in Memphis, south-west of the main Ptah temple. However, by the Ptolemaic period his cult had spread south to Thebes where provision was made for his worship in the Temple of Ptah at Karnak. In the reign of the Roman Emperor Tiberius an elaborate eulogy to Imhotep was carved on the fourth gate before his temple. He shared honours at Thebes with Amenhotep son of Hapu, a deified 'Director of all royal works' who had lived in the reign of the pharaoh Amenhotep III (1403–1365 BC). At the temple of Deir el-Medina in Western Thebes, Imhotep is depicted with his mythical mother Khereduankh, in the guise of the goddess Hathor. To complete the sacred triad of which the Egyptians were so fond, he is given a wife who is called 'God's sister', Renpet-nefret.

As his cult spread, more and more emphasis was placed on his role as a supreme physician readily identifiable with the Greek Asklepios. This aspect was particularly prominent in his Ptolemaic sanctuary in Western Thebes, on the upper terrace of Queen Hatshepsut's temple at Deir el-Bahri, as well as in the Temple of Hathor at Dendera, where an important eulogy to Imhotep connects him by inference to the sanatorium there. Elsewhere we find attempts to enhance his deification such as at one town in the Delta where, in a development reminiscent of the elevation of the statues of the Virgin Mary under early theologians, Khereduankh the mother of Imhotep becomes regarded as the offspring of a god, in this case Banebdjedet, the sacred ram-deity of Mendes.

The cult of Imhotep became a focal point for married couples desiring a son. A good example of his procreative powers is carved on perhaps the most poignant stela in the British Museum's collection. It is the autobiography of a woman called Taimhotep who was born in 73 BC during the reign of Ptolemy XII Neos Dionysos. When she was fourteen, she married Psherenptah, High Priest of Ptah of Memphis. Three pregnancies produced daughters. Together, Taimhotep and Psherenptah prayed to Imohtep son of Ptah for a son. Imhotep appeared to Psherenptah in a dream or revelation with a proposal: a major embellishment to his sanctuary in Ankh-tawi (the Memphite necropolis where Imhotep was buried) in exchange for a male child. Psherenptah consequently commissioned a gold statue and dedicated it to Imhotep's sanctuary, whereupon Taimhotep conceived a son. On the Feast of Imhotep in 46 BC Taimhotep gave birth to Pedibast. The rewards of motherhood were short-lived, however, because Taimhotep died in 42 BC when she was thirty. The rest of the stela comprises a moving lament on the inevitability of death. Despite this, Imhotep's positive intervention had changed the couple's life. It was this immediacy of Imhotep son of Ptah as resolver of human problems, often medical, that ensured the popularity of his cult into the Roman period.

Commander Djeheuty

The military campaigns of the pharaoh Tuthmosis III (1490–1439 BC) established Egyptian authority either by occupation-forces or by favourable trading tactics over an area stretching from the Sudan to Syria. In particular his battle against a Middle-Eastern confederacy in front of the Canaanite city of Megiddo and the subsequent seven-month siege brought about the capitulation of 330 enemy princes. But the pharaoh was still compelled to make regular parades of military might in the Levant and continual punitive strikes against Syrian armies. Occasionally we learn about his military personnel, such as Amenemhab who killed the elephant that threatened the king's life in a hunt near the Euphrates.

Likewise, we can assume that Garrison Commander Djeheuty was an acclaimed warrior on the pharaoh's general staff. Inscriptions from his Theban tomb give an idea of his historical status:

King's follower in every foreign land ... overseer of northern countries ... supplier of storehouses with lapis lazuli, silver and gold.

Accordingly his career as a governor in the Middle East was at a time of maximum Egyptian sovereignty and control of foreign wealth – lapis lazuli came via trade-routes from Afghanistan and silver from mines in Anatolia. His posthumous fame led to him becoming the hero of an escapade set in the time of Tuthmosis III's conquests but one which is probably quite fictional.

The source for the tale is a Ramesside papyrus in the British Museum written at least 150 years after Djeheuty's death.

The setting is an Egyptian siege of the port of Joppa on the coast of Palestine. Djeheuty is in conference with the Prince of Joppa in an attempt to persuade him that he, Djeheuty, intends to turn traitor and, together with his wife and children, come over to the enemy camp. As proof of Djeheuty's sincerity the Prince of Joppa demands to see the sceptre of authority of Tuthmosis III kept in the Egyptian High Command's tent. Djeheuty brings the sceptre but only to deliver the Prince of Joppa a stunning blow on the head. He then binds him in metal fetters. The ruse now adopted by Djeheuty has great similarity to the tale of *Ali Baba and the Forty Thieves*. Djeheuty organises 200 soldiers with fetters and bonds to be carried in 200 sealed baskets by 500 troops. Their orders are to enter Joppa and fetter its inhabitants. Djeheuty arranges for false information to be passed on to the herald of the Prince of Joppa to the effect that the Prince's forces have captured Djeheuty and his family, and that the 200 baskets are part of the tribute now destined for the city. This message is taken to the Princess of Joppa who gives orders for the city gates to be opened to admit the 200 baskets. The Egyptian troops then overrun Joppa and take its inhabitants as prisoners, bound in fetters. The papyrus closes with Djeheuty writing a letter to Tuthmosis III informing him of the victory which he suggests should be used to fill the Temple of Amun-Re with slaves.

Ramesses II and the Princess of Hatti

From the Nile Delta down to Nubia, temples, statues and stelae will not let you forget that Egypt was once ruled by Ramesses II (1290–1224 BC). His Delta residence was in fact so opulent that it inspired eulogies:

... The sun rises and sets within its limits. Its west is the Temple of Amun, its south the Temple of Seth, the goddess Astarte shines in its east and the goddess Wadjet appears in its north.

On the walls and pylons of most of his temples you can read in scenes and in hieroglyph the official version of the pharaoh's battle against the Hittities at Kadesh on the River Orontes in 1285 BC. But despite the propaganda-machine extolling his prowess it is clear that his intention to dislodge the Hittites from Syria and north Lebanon had failed. After a cold war both Hittites and Egyptians agreed on a non-aggression pact, officially sealed in the names of the deities of each state in 1269 BC. Thirteen years later stelae at Karnak, Elephantine and Abu Simbel proclaim an international wedding between Ramesses II and the daughter of the Great Prince of Hatti (the Hittite king). However, the two arch enemies are now fully reconciled by a legal treaty and a diplomatic marriage. The Egyptian account pretends that the Great Prince of Hatti, attributing drought in his land to the influence of Ramasses II with the Hittite storm god, decides to send his daughter and

Granite head and shoulders of the pharaoh Ramesses II (1290–1224 BC) whose alliance with the Hittites was strengthened by a diplomatic marriage.

limitless tribute to Egypt. The pharaoh intercedes with the god Seth to keep storms out of the skies during the princess's journey. On her arrival in Egypt Ramesses II was struck by her beauty. He announced that her status was to be 'King's wife, Maat-nefru-Re'. She appears to have been joined by a second Hittite princess, who became another wife of Ramesses II, and she ended her days in the Royal Harem in the Faiyum province.

A thousand years after the historical marriage we can follow Ramesses II and Queen Maat-nefru-Re into legend via a Ptolemaic stela in the Louvre Museum. It was discovered in a now-vanished sanctuary near the Temple of Khonsu at Karnak and was a forgery by the priests who knew the historical facts of the Hittite princess, even remembering an element of her Egyptian name. The purpose of the stela seems to have been twofold: to emphasise the hierarchical order of the two forms of the god Khonsu and, in the face of the recent Persian and Greek conquests of Egypt, to indulge in subtle nationalism by setting the tale in the era of Ramesses II when a native-born Egyptian pharaoh ruled the country.

The stela begins with a conflation of the royal titulary of Ramesses II and Tuthmosis IV. Ramesses II is then said to be in Naharin, a region in the Upper Euphrates. Historically, Ramesses II had never emulated the achievements of Tuthmosis I and Tuthmosis III who set up stelae on the banks of the Euphrates, since the Hittites thwarted his ambitions in North Syria at the battle of Kudesh. However, in the stela, Ramesses II receives tribute of precious metal, lapis lazuli, turquoise and valuable timber. The Prince of Bakhtan set his daughter at the head of his tribute. The location of Bakhtan might be purely imaginary but a good case has been made for its identification with Bactria. Ramesses II is captivated by her beauty and bestows on her the title 'Great Royal Wife, Nefru-Re'.

Later, Ramesses II was celebrating the 'Beautiful Festival of the Valley' in honour of Amun-Re at Thebes when a messenger from Bakhtan arrives with presents for Queen Nefru-Re. He also brings bad news about the Queen's younger sister who was dangerously ill. Her name is given as Bentresh, which may be part Egyptian and part Canaanite and means 'Daughter of Joy'. This would be analogous to the actual name of Ramesses II's daughter-wife Bint-Anat. Ramesses II summons the research-fellows in the House of Life and his palace staff, all in all an assembly of his top academics, physicians and magicians. The Royal Scribe Djeheuty-em-hab is selected to go to Bakhtan to ascertain Princess Bentresh's malady. (Egyptian doctors had a wide reputation in the ancient Near East – in the fact in the Persian dominion of Egypt shortly before this stela was composed the chief physician Wadjahorresne spent time at the court of King Darius I in Iran.) Djeheuty-em-hab diagnoses that Bentresh is possessed by hostile spirits and that only a god could contend with them. Bakhtan is so remote that it is nearly three years after the news of the sickness of Princess Bentresh first reached Ramesses II that the request for divine assistance comes to him.

At this point the god Khonsu, son of Amun-Re and Mut, is consulted by Ramesses who makes a plea for Bentresh. The first and most senior form of Khonsu is 'Khonsu in Thebes Nefer-hotep'. However, the priests manipulate matters such that the response comes from a specialised manifestation of the god, called 'Khonsu-fulfiller-of-schemes', whose skill lay in expelling 'disease-demons'. From ritual inclinations (noddings) of the god's statue, the decision is taken to send 'Khonsu-fulfiller-of-schemes', protected by magical amulets from the senior Khonsu, in a great flotilla together with horses and chariots to Bakhtan. When the god reaches Bentresh seventeen months later his power to cure is immediate and the princess recovers fully. The major spirit which had caused her illness now acknowledges the supremacy of Khonsu and, surprisingly, persuades the god to make the Prince of Bakhtan initiate a feast day in his (i.e. the spirit's) honour.

The Prince of Bakhtan then becomes reluctant to let the god's statue leave and he keeps it in his country for three years and nine months. But he then has a dream in which the god, in the form of a golden falcon, appears to come at him from his shrine and soar up into the sky in the direction of Egypt. The Prince realises his mistake and sends the statue back to Thebes with great tribute. On arrival, 'Khonsu-fulfiller-of-schemes' presents these gifts from Bakhtan to the senior 'Khonsu in Thebes Nefer-hotep' – minus a few items which his priesthood kept as commission for the arduous journey.

Tales of fantasy

The stories in this section have been chosen as examples of how wonders of magic, exotic location and extraordinary adventures provided an excellent vehicle for scribes to structure an escape from routine life. Although the contents of these papyri are a valued legacy of Ancient Egyptian literature, their origins lie in the repertoire of storytellers. The oral traditions from which they grew were the entertainment/media of Egyptian villagers. The tales might become most elaborate under scribal editing but the humble sources from which they sprang were never scorned. The vizier Ptahhotep, the author of a wisdom text, *Instruction of Ptahhotep*, in about 2400 BC, comments: 'the art of good speech is certainly a rarity but that does not rule out your discovery of it in the mouths of the women who turn grindstones'.

A cycle of tales of magic set in the Pyramid Era in early Dynasty IV (*c.* 2550 BC) are preserved in Berlin Papyrus 3033, popularly known as the Westcar Papyrus after the English traveller who acquired them on his visit to Egypt in 1823–4. The language of the document is classical Middle Kingdom Egyptian (*c.* 2040–*c.* 1783 BC), although the papyrus itself is a slightly later copy which dates to the early sixteenth century BC. The strong historical context of this cycle of legends is embroidered by the scribe with the entertainment centred around great magicians whose fame had lasted nearly a thousand years by the time the papyrus was written. There were originally five tales but the first one is all but lost and the second is woefully fragmentary. So we begin with the third tale where Baufre, son of King Khufu (*r. c.* 2550 BC), builder of the Great Pyramid at Giza, is about to relate a wonder performed by a magician in the reign of King Sneferu, Khufu's father.

Djadja-em-ankh and his power over water

On one occasion King Sneferu – a pharaoh well documented in historical inscriptions and a prolific constructor of pyramids at Meidum and Dahshur – wanders around his palace frustrated with boredom. He sends for Djadja-em-ankh, his chief lector-priest. In ancient Egypt this title literally read: 'The one who carries the ritual book'; in other words, an official designated to hold ceremonial papyri, normally in a religious or funerary context. This may have been when pronouncing liturgy in a temple, or when reciting the spell for 'opening the mouth', at the tombside where the mummified corpse has living faculties magically restored to it.

In this particular instance, however, Djadja-em-ankh has the role of court magician whose secret spells are contained in the papyrus which he holds. Sneferu asks his magician for some ideas on alleviating his ennui. Djadja-em-ankh suggests that the king needs a breath of fresh air in the delightful environment of the palace lake where wildfowl and scenery would combine to cheer him up, especially if some beautiful girls from the royal harem rowed across the lake in front of him. The king thinks this a brilliant idea and organises a boat to be filled with twenty girls who have not born children, whose hair is finely braided and whose figures are curvaceous. Even more exciting to the king's mind is his own instruction that instead of their normal linen dresses the girls would wear only nets of faience beads. They are given oars that have been overlaid with gold leaf and start to row up and down in front of the pharaoh.

All goes well until the lead stroke, playing with her braided hair, loses her hair-clasp pendant of high-quality turquoise in the lake. (Some of these fish-shaped hair pendants survive in museum collections.) Upset, she stops rowing and so causes the boat to come to a halt. When Sneferu finds out what has happened, he offers to replace the lost pendant so that the rowing can continue. We know that he sent expeditions to the turquoise mining region of Maghara in the Sinai peninsula and so had a fair supply. Using a colloquial expression, the girl replies: 'I prefer my pot to one like it', meaning that she considers the lost turquoise to have been of exceptional quality, not to be matched. Rather petulantly King Sneferu turns to his magician and more or less tells him that since the outing was his idea he can solve the dilemma. Obediently Djadja-em-ankh does so by reciting a magic spell (which, infuriatingly, the papyrus does not divulge). The lake is over 6 m deep and upon the magic words half of it rises up to form a wall of water over 12 m high, revealing the lake bottom and the pendant. Djadja-em-ankh retrieves it and restores it to the girl. With another magical utterance he restores the lake to its previous condition. All this excitement becomes an excuse for a celebratory feast and Djadja-em-ankh is well rewarded for his magical powers.

Djedi and his power to restore life

In the next tale Prince Hordedef, another son of Khufu, and one who posthumously had a reputation as the wise author of a book of instructions on life, tells his father of the amazing magical skill of one of his own subjects. Khufu is intrigued, especially when he learns that this magician, called Djedi, knows about the secret apartments in the sanctuary of Thoth, god of wisdom, because Khufu himself had been trying to find out about them in order to make an architectural replica in one of his own temples. Consequently Prince Hordedef sails south from Memphis to the town of Djed-Sneferu where Djedi lives. Djedi is in good health and has a tremendous appetite – 500 loaves a day plus half an ox and 100 jugs of beer – not bad for someone who had reached the age of 110 (a model age among ancient Egyptians). When the prince arrives, in a splendid sedan chair, Djedi is stretched out on a mat in front of his house having an oil-massage. After an elaborate exchange of courtesies, he gathers together his valuable scrolls and sets off with Hordedef for the royal residence.

Djedi enters the main court of the palace and is received by King Khufu, who is eager to see him perform some of the spectacular magic involving the reunion of dismembered bodies that he has been told about. Djedi agrees to perform and Khufu quite callously gives orders for a prisoner to be brought as the assistant. Here Djedi quickly displays his humanity by refusing to perform on a human being, protesting that mankind are 'illustrious cattle', a reference to the concept that the human race is the herd of the creator god. As a result a goose is chosen. It is decapitated and its head placed at the eastern side of the court, its body at the west. Djedi utters his magic spell, which again we are not able to read. The goose's body waddles across to its head, which is also animated, and they join together and start to honk. Similar successes are achieved in the case of a wading water-fowl (perhaps a flamingo) and an ox. Unfortunately an earlier reference to Djedi being able to tame a wild lion to walk behind him is not developed by the scribe of this papyrus.

Khufu now broaches the subject of the number of secret apartments in the sanctuary of Thoth. Djedi denies knowing the answer himself, but says it can be found in a chest in a storeroom in the sanctuary of the sun god at Heliopolis. Furthermore, Djedi is not destined to be the one to bring the chest to the palace.

The tale now incorporates a prophecy concerning a future change of royal family, which in history we recognise as the emergence of Dynasty V in about 2465 BC. Djedi tells King Khufu that the chest will be retrieved by Ruddedet, the wife of a priest of the sun god who will bear three children sired by Re himself. The throne of Egypt will pass to them. Khufu becomes depressed at these words but Djedi encourages him by revealing that Khufu's son and grandson will inherit the throne before the prophecy comes to pass. (Historically the succession of the throne in Dynasty IV was more complex than Djedi's prophecy – the papyrus ignores the problem of Radjedef, Khufu's immediate successor, who built his pyramid at Abu Rawesh north of Giza, and seemingly regards the last ruler, Shepseskaf, as too insignificant to count.) Ruddedet will give birth, states Djedi, in early winter when the Nile flood has receded. Khufu, who wants to visit a major sanctuary of Re at Sakhbu to commemorate the birth, to which he seems reconciled, tells Djedi that the journey will be hampered since the 'Two-Fish Nile branch' in the Delta which he has to negotiate will be empty. Djedi informs Khufu that his magic will cause about 2 m of water to appear in the dried-up canal, so that the visit will not be impeded. The reward for Djedi's skill in magic and prophecy is to be given a place in the royal household with Prince Hordedef and with vastly increased food rations.

The enchanted island

This tale is normally called by egyptologists *The Shipwrecked Sailor* but the ancient scribe definitely put its emphasis more on the exotic location of the mysterious island and on the supernatural creature living there. The source of this adventure is a papyrus in the Moscow Museum which dates to the Middle Kingdom, the classical era of Egyptian literature. (It probably dates in particular to some time in the nineteenth century BC). It is relevant that this period of Egyptian civilisation witnessed the expansion of pharaonic power in Nubia, south of the granite frontier at Aswan. There was an intensification of control over the goldmines, with massive fortresses being constructed around the Second Cataract of the Nile. In addition there was a spirit of exploration involving royal agents being sent into the Sudan to investigate lucrative trade routes.

At the beginning of *The Enchanted Island* an unnamed envoy is returning from an exploratory trade mission in Nubia. From historical inscriptions, like the autobiography of Governor Harkhuf (about 2240 BC) carved on the front of his tomb at Qubbet el-Hawa at Aswan, we know the luxury goods which would be looked for by the pharaoh – incense, ebony, elephant tusks and panther skins. The envoy is in an acute state of depression because he has clearly been unsuccessful on the expedition and he is worried how to explain his boat empty of valuables to the king. One man in his entourage – the actual 'shipwrecked sailor' of the story – exhorts him to look on the bright side. The expedition has suffered no loss of life *en route* and is now safely out of Nubia on the Egyptian side of the First Cataract. The sailor insists on telling the envoy a yarn about an adventure he once had.

He was on an expedition bound for the royal mines, using a route that involved navigating on the Red Sea. The boat was impressive, being 60 m long and 40 m wide. His companions (there were 120 sailors altogether) were fearless, unintimidated by the natural elements and able to foretell when a storm was brewing. But a too sudden squall brought a 4 m-high wave so that – as the papyrus says – 'the boat died'. All the crew were lost at sea with the exception of himself who was cash ashore on an island.

For three days he hid under the protection of trees until his thirst drove him to explore the island. He found he had been shipwrecked in a veritable Garden of Eden – he was surrounded by ripe figs, grapes, vegetables and cucumbers and an abundance of fish and wildfowl. Having eaten to excess, he then lit a fire and made a burnt-offering to the gods to show his gratitude for having survived. Obviously the smoke gave away his whereabouts because the trees promptly started to crash to the ground and the island seemed to shudder. To his consternation he saw a gigantic snake about 16 m long approaching. It was a creature of legend: covered in gold scales, it had eyebrows made of lapis lazuli and, like a god, it wore a beard which hung down a metre.

The snake, which had the power of human speech, reared up and demanded an explanation from the sailor as to how he had come to the island. The accompanying threat that if the answer was not given quickly the snake would spit flames and reduce the sailor to ashes left the latter incoherent with terror. So the snake became more benign and carried the sailor in its jaws without injury to its dwelling. Reassured, the sailor related the story of the shipwreck (in an account which is almost verbatim the original description – a feature common to the oral tradition of poetry or story-telling). The snake told the sailor that a divine force had drawn him to the 'island of the Ka'. This phrase is difficult to translate – the 'Ka' is the life-force of a person born at the same time as the physical body but surviving physical death as a spiritual entity. One egyptologist has suggested that 'phantom island' might be a possible rendering. However, since the 'Ka' is a magical power, capable of bringing to reality inanimate representations of, for example, bread, beer jugs, incense, linen clothing and animals, then 'the Enchanted Island' is probably the snake's meaning. The sailor was then told that his sojourn on the island would last four months, until his friends would sail past and rescue him. The snake emphasised that the sailor would reach home and die in his own town. Burial in Egypt was of paramount importance since only then would the correct funerary rituals be performed. Also the snake pointed out that the experience of a calamity could be compensated by the feelings of relief when the situation had improved.

The next development is that the snake gives his own story within the framework of the sailor's tale, which in turn is a diversion for the low spirits of the envoy. This storyteller's ruse of tales within tales, occurring here in a simple form nearly 4,000 years ago, is the basis for some of the most elaborate concoctions of Princess Scheherazade in *The Arabian Nights' Entertainments*. On the Enchanted Island there were originally seventy-five snakes. One day all the others were killed by a falling star (this was probably a reference to a meteorite) which burned them up in flames. The one surviving snake was desolated but eventually overcame his grief. However, to the sailor he reflects on the contentment of family life. Moved by his tale, the sailor avows that on his return to Egypt he will proclaim the magnanimity of the snake to strangers like himself and send a cargo of exotic goods such as fragrant oil and myrrh to the island. The snake in laughter replies that the island has more valuable produce than the sailor could ever hope to see. He calls himself the 'Prince of Punt' – the land from where Egypt obtained incense, goods and produce of Equatorial Africa, situated in the region of the River Atbara – and moreover, once the sailor has gone away the island will disappear below the waves of the Red Sea. (Of course by this clever device the storyteller ensured that no-one could be so prosaic as to check out the facts of the sailor's yarn.)

Four months later a boat with a crew of his friends approached close by the island and was hailed by the sailor who had climbed a high tree. The benevolent snake sped him on his way with a gift of a rich cargo consisting of myrrh, oil, perfumed unguent, eye paint, giraffe tails, elephant tusks,

Tribute from Nubia of the sort referred to by the sailor and the gigantic serpent in the tale of the enchanted island. Note in particular the giraffe with the monkey climbing up its neck. Tomb of Rekhmire, Western Thebes, c. 1450 BC.

greyhounds, monkeys and baboons. On the West Bank at Thebes, if you look at the walls of Queen Hatshepsut's temple at Deir el-Bahari and of the rock tomb of the vizier Rekhmire, you can see exactly this kind of produce coming from southern countries into Egypt. Two months later – with the switch from the Red Sea to the River Nile glossed over – the sailor reached the royal residence and handed over his goods. He was rewarded by the pharaoh with an endowment of serfs and was made a palace official. The irony of the successful outcome of the sailor's adventure, in contrast to the dismal failure of the envoy to whom the tale has been told, makes for a sardonic ending. The envoy uses an analogy between the futility of giving water at dawn to a goose that is going to be slaughtered later in the morning and in his own case the hopelessness of being cheered up briefly before facing the pharaoh.

To indicate that the conclusion of the tale has been reached the papyrus finishes with the words: 'It has come from its beginning to its end just as found in the writing – the work of the scribe excellent of fingers, Imeny's son Imen-aa, may he live may he prosper may he be healthy'.

The metamorphoses of Bata

In the British Museum there is a papyrus (no. 10183) commonly referred to as the *Tale of the Two Brothers*, immaculately written in the Hieratic script by the scribe Inena who lived around the last quarter of the thirteenth century BC. It is an intricate concoction of mythology, folklore and humour. Although some of the events might seem far-fetched, we are never remote from human emotions and foibles.

Two brothers, Anubis (the elder) and Bata live in the same house. (The fact that they bear the names of Egyptian deities vaguely connects them with the world of myth through the legend of the Jackal Nome of Upper Egypt as it survives in a later and complex document known as Papyrus Jumilhac.) Anubis has a wife who is regrettably never named. Bata lives with them but sleeps in the cattle stable and acts as a general handyman in making clothes for Anubis and in bearing the brunt of agricultural work. His unfailing strength has gained him a good reputation. He has the gift of understanding the speech of the cattle which he tends so that when they tell him 'The grass of such-and-such a place is delicious' he takes them there to graze. This gives good results in terms of increased calving.

One day in the ploughing season when the brothers are sowing barley and emmer-seed in the fields, the supply runs out. Bata is sent to fetch some more. He finds his brother's wife braiding her hair and rather peremptorily asks her to get up and give him a supply of seed as quickly as possible. Not surprisingly, she tells him not to interrupt her coiffure session and to go to the storage bin to collect the seed himself. Bata takes a large jar to carry the maximum amount of seed. His brother's wife inquires how much he is carrying, to which he answers 'Three sacks of barley and two of emmer-wheat'. This would be an impressive load equivalent to eleven bushels. His brother's wife becomes sexually stimulated at seeing his energy. She grabs hold of Bata, suggesting that there is now an opportunity to sleep together for an hour. It will be good for him, she asserts, and she will undertake to make him fine linen clothes. Bata's moral behaviour finds this proposition horrific and he becomes as fierce as a leopard in his rage. It is unacceptable to entertain such an iniquitous idea since he lives like a son with her and his older brother. However, he promises that the matter will be divulged to no-one and returns to Anubis in the fields. In the evening Bata sets off to sleep in his cattle stable.

In an episode illustrating the ingenuity of Anubis' wife, Bata pays a terrible price for scorning her proposition. Before Anubis returns his wife makes herself look as though she has been viciously assaulted. Instead of lighting a fire she leaves the house in darkness, perplexing Anubis on his arrival. Her normal custom is to pour water over her husband's hands when he comes home but she does not on this occasion. Instead, Anubis finds her on her bed looking distraught and in a fit of vomiting (cleverly brought on by swallowing fat and grease). Perhaps the shock of seeing his wife so distressed numbs Anubis into the inane inquiry: 'Who has been speaking with you?' His wife immediately launches into a devastating character-assassination of Bata, reversing the actual happening. She tells Anubis that his younger brother suggested that she untied her hair braids and joined him in bed for an hour. From her story it is she who protested that they were like a mother and father to him upon which he became scared at what he had proposed and beat her to stop her talking to Anubis. She challenges her husband to kill Bata, otherwise she will die.

Anubis now displays his anger. As Bata has not yet arrived home with the cattle, Anubis hides behind the stable door with his spear in hand, ready to kill him. It is the first cow in the line approaching the stable who saves Bata's life with a warning about Anubis hiding there armed with his spear. Bata catches a glimpse of his brother's feet and escapes in flight with Anubis in hot pursuit. A prayer for justice to the sun god Re-Horakhti results in the god creating an expanse of water full of crocodiles to separate the two brothers and to keep Bata safe until the following dawn. From safety, Bata vigorously protests his innocence to Anubis, describing the real sequence of events. He accuses his brother of being ready to spear him on he uncorroborated testimony of a despicable harlot. He drastically backs up his oath of truthfulness to Re-Harahkti by cutting off his phallus with a reed-knife. He throws it into the water where it becomes a morsel of food for a catfish. Gradually growing weaker through loss of blood Bata arouses the pity of his brother who stands there in tears, frustrated from reaching the bank where Bata stands because of the crocodiles.

In a last speech to Anubis, Bata asserts that he cannot remain but will go the Valley of the Pine. If this location was intended to conjure up an actual geographical region then it would be in the Lebanon. Bata states that he will take out his own heart and place it on the top of a pine flower. (How he is to survive without it is not developed in the text.) He requests that Anubis comes to search for him if the pine tree is cut down – for that will result in the death of Bata – and rescue his heart. If Anubis puts Bata's heart in a bowl of water then Bata will exact revenge on the person who killed him. The sign Anubis will receive if calamity strikes Bata will be a jug of beer suddenly fermenting in his hand. Bata departs for the Valley of the Pine while Anubis, smeared with dust to show his grief, journeys home. He kills his wife and unceremoniously throws her corpse to scavenging dogs.

Meanwhile Bata, his heart on the top of the pine flower in the Valley of the Pine, builds a villa where he lives alone. The bizarre scenario so far has merely been the platform for taking off into a flight of total fantasy. Bata encounters the Ennead of the sun god who are the governors of this region as well as of Egypt. The Ennead inform Bata that he is vindicated in his reputation and blameless of any wrongdoing. Moreover, Anubis has killed the woman who was the cause of the whole business. To relieve his loneliness Re-Harakhti instructs the god Khnum to make Bata a wife. Khnum moulds a ravishingly beautiful woman in whose body is the essence of the gods themselves. In view of the consequential disasters which she causes Bata there seems more than a fleeting similarity with the Greek legend of Pandora, fashioned by Hephaistos on the orders of Zeus to be a blight to mankind. When Khnum has finished carving Bata's wife (another nameless woman) the Seven Hathors, goddesses connected with destiny, foretell that she will come to a violent death. We cannot ignore the anomalous marital relationship now brought into being for the self-castrated Bata and a sexually attractive woman.

One day Bata gives away the secret to his wife that his heart rests on the top of a pine flower. This is to be his undoing. He tells her because he worries that if she walks on the seashore, she may be swept away. He has to admit that his vulnerability might prevent him rescuing her. Shortly after this warning, and while Bata is away hunting in the desert, the sea surges after his wife while she is out walking. She escapes into the villa but the pine next to the villa traps a scented lock of her hair on behalf of the sea which washes it upon the shore of Egypt where pharaoh's launderers carry out their work. The perfume of the hair permeates all the linen garments which are being washed and the pharaoh complains about the scent. Eventually the chief laundryman discovers the lock of hair. The meaning of the situation is interpreted by the scribes: the lock of hair imbued with the gods' essence belongs to a daughter of Re-Harakhti and has come to Egypt to encourage the pharaoh to search for her and fetch her from the Valley of the Pine. The first expedition of troops sent to bring the woman to Egypt are all slaughtered by Bata in the Valley of the Pine. The next expedition of troops and chariots is accompanied by a woman whose task is to entice Bata's wife with exquisite jewellery to leave her restricted life in Lebanon for the sophisti-cation of the Egyptian royal court. The plan succeeds and Bata's wife comes to Egypt where she is loved by the pharaoh and given exalted status in the palace. The pharaoh learns about the heart of Bata on the pine flower and gives orders for the pine tree to be cut down. At that moment, Bata drops down dead.

The next day Anubis discovers his beer fermenting in its jug and recog-nises the sign of calamity about which Bata had spoken. He journeys to the Valley of the Pine and finds Bata lying dead in his villa. The search for Bata's heart takes just over three years and Anubis eventually discovers it disguised as a fruit to keep it safe. He puts it in a bowl of water and Bata's body begins to twitch. Anubis touches Bata's lips with water, Bata drinks some more, and his heart is restored to him.

Bata's metamorphoses so far have been from a virile young man to a eunuch and a corpse, but more are to come. He wants revenge on his wife and decides to travel to Egypt in the form of a strikingly coloured bull. Anubis rides on the bull's back and they both go to the royal residence. The pharaoh is captivated immediately by the beauty of the bull and rewards Anubis with gold and silver. Bata the bull is fêted and fussed over by the pharaoh. One day the bull confronts the wife of his former human self. He terrifies her when he reveals that he is Bata seeking revenge for her act of causing the pine tree to be cut down. He leaves, but his wife schemes a way of destroying this threat to her security. When the pharaoh is 'in his cups' after a delectable feast, she extracts from him a promise to let her eat the liver of Bata the bull. Later, the pharaoh regrets his promise but is as powerless to change it as Herod, captivated by Salome, was to rescind the order for John the Baptist's execution. The next day Bata the bull is slaughtered as a sacrificial offering, but as the men carry the body by the king's great gateway Bata causes two drops of blood to fall from his severed throat. During the night two huge Persea trees grow by the gateway. The pharaoh considers this propitious and a celebration is made in their honour.

A long while afterwards the pharaoh makes an official appearance at his 'Window of Appearances' – a ceremonial dais of which a well-preserved example survives as the link between the palace and mortuary temple of Rameses III at Medinet Habu on the West Bank at Thebes. Then with Bata's wife, now his principal queen, he drives in a golden chariot to inspect the Persea trees. While the royal couple are relaxing in their shade Bata reveals to his wife that he has metamorphosed from the bull into the Persea trees and is still very much alive and intent on revenge. The woman once again uses her charms and guile to get the pharaoh to agree to fell the Persea trees and make them into furniture. While she is watching the carpenters carry out the king's instructions a splinter is struck off and flies into the mouth of Bata's wife. She immediately becomes pregnant and in due course gives birth to a son who is, unbeknown to all, none other than her previous husband Bata. The pharaoh is over the moon with joy. The reborn Bata is honoured as he grows up, given the title of 'King's son of Kush', which makes him responsible for the vast gold resources of Nubia, and he is acclaimed as heir-apparent. When the pharaoh dies Bata ascends the throne and calls together the great officials of Egypt. He relates his adventures and metamorphoses. Then his 'wife-mother' is brought in and the magistrates agree in judgement upon her. Just as happens in the historical 'conspiracy papyrus' in the Turin Museum where the fate of a queen of Ramesses III, guilty of plotting to kill the king and put her son on the throne, is not specified, so the description of the judgement on Bata's wife is vague. In both cases, however, execution or invitation to suicide is certainly the sentence. Anubis becomes crown prince and when Bata, after a reign of thirty years, finally dies – without emerging in a new form in this world – it is his older brother who assumes the kingship of Egypt.

Suggestions for further reading

The soundest way to get to grips with the complexities of Egyptian mythology is to immerse yourself in modern literal translations of ancient original documents. Reliable translations of many of the sources for the myths and legends discussed in this book can be found in J. B. Pritchard (ed.), *Ancient Near Eastern Texts relating to the old testament* (3rd edn with supplement), Princeton University Press 1969 and in M. Lichteim, *Ancient Egyptian Literature* (3 vols covering the Old Kingdom to the Late Period), University of California Press 1973, 1976, 1980. For attempts to synthesise the salient features of Egyptian religion in one book I would recommend E. Hornung, *Conceptions of God in Ancient Egypt – The One and the Many*, Routledge and Kegan Paul 1983, and S. Morenz, *Egyptian Religion*, Methuen 1973. Also as a quick reference to the essential nature of the deities figuring in these myths you can consult G. Hart, *Dictionary of Egyptian Gods and Goddesses*, Routledge and Kegan Paul 1986.

The chapters concerning the structure of the cosmos and the transition of the throne of Egypt from Osiris to Horus might be followed up by reading the following major sources: R. O. Faulkner, *The Ancient Egyptian Pyramid Texts*, Oxford University Press 1969 and R. O. Faulkner, *The Ancient Egyptian Coffin Texts* (3 vols), Aris and Phillips 1973, 1977, 1987. The Edfu drama concerning Horus' annihilation of Seth can be found in H. W. Fairman, *The Triumph of Horus*, Batsford 1974. Erudite observations on the myth of kingship abound in J. Gwyn-Griffiths, *Plutarch's De Iside et Osiride*, University of Wales 1970. For stimulating discussions both on cosmology and kingship you can turn to J. R. Allen, *Genesis in Egypt – The Philosophy of Ancient Egyptian Creation Accounts*, Yale University 1988 and H. Frankfort, *Kingship and the Gods – A study of Near Eastern religion as the integration of society and nature*, University of Chicago Press 1948. For the study of Isis as supreme font of magical power the original spells are the most rewarding for initial research and are gathered in J. F. Bourghouts, *Ancient Egyptian Magical Texts*, E. J. Brill 1978.

You should now plunge deep into the rich imagery of the Egyptian underworld, translated and lavishly illustrated in A. Piankoff, *The Tomb of Ramesses* VI (2 vols), Pantheon Books 1954. The best book on the Theban royal tombs to complement underworld studies is E. Hornung, *Tal der Könige – Die Ruhestätte der Pharaonen*, Artemis 1988. The afterlife of non-royal mortals is readily accessible in R. O. Faulkner, (ed. C. A. R. Andrews), *The Ancient Egyptian Book of the Dead*, British Museum Publications 1989. To pursue further some of the notable persons who became deified or entered the world of legends you can consult D. Wildung, *Egyptian Saints – Deification in Pharaonic Egypt*, New York University Press 1977, or his more careful and scholarly, *Imhotep und Amenhotep*, Munich 1977.

Finally, no civilisation documented its beliefs so visually as the ancient Egyptians. For fine illustrations of some of the myths and deities in this book you can browse with pleasure over the plates in E. Otto, *Egyptian Art and the cults of Osiris and Amun*, Thames and Hudson 1968, and in E. Brunner-Traut, (*et al.*) *Osiris Kreuz und Halbmond*, Philipp von Zabern, Muinz am Rhein 1984.

Index and picture credits

Picture credits

Photographs have been supplied by courtesy of the British Museum or by the following: *front cover:* Peter Webb; *pp. 8, 23, 31, 43 (right):* The Metropolitan Museum of Art, New York: Rogers Fund and Henry Walters Gift, 1916 (16.1.3); Gift of Edward S. Harkness, 1926 (26.7.1412); Rogers Fund, 1945 (45.2.11); Fletcher Fund, 1950 (50.85); *p. 12:* Museo Egizio, Torino; *p. 14:* Musée du Louvre, Paris; *pp. 17, 51 (bottom), 54:* Franco Maria Ricci editore, Milano, from *Nella Sede della Verità* by A. Fornari and M. Tosi (photo: Franco Lovera, Torino).

Quotations used in the text are reprinted by permission of the following:

pp. 7, 61 Faber and Faber Ltd from 'Little Gidding' from *Four Quartets* by T.S. Eliot and from *Collected Poems 1909–1962* by T.S. Eliot; *p.19* Routledge and Kegan-Paul; *p.28* Oxford University Press; *p.53* Princeton University Press.